Experiencing Bereavement

Helen Alexander

Pauline
BOOKS & MEDIA
Boston

Library of Congress Cataloging-in-Publication Data

Alexander, Helen Mae.

  Experiencing bereavement / by Helen Alexander.— 3rd ed.

    p. cm.

Includes bibliographical references.

  ISBN 0-8198-2353-8 (pbk.)

  1. Bereavement—Religious aspects—Christianity. I. Title.

  BV4905.3 .A44 2003

  248.8'66—dc22

                              2003019884

Cover art: Dynamic Graphics

Cover design: Regina Frances Dick, FSP

2003 Printed and published in the U.S.A. by Pauline Books & Media, 50 Saint Paul's Avenue, Boston, MA 02130-3491.

www.pauline.org

Pauline Books & Media is the publishing house of the Daughters of St. Paul, an international congregation of women religious serving the Church with the communications media.

1 2 3 4 5 6 7 8 9   11 10 09 08 07 06 05 04 03

To Ruth and Callum

Contents

Preface

Everyone's experience of bereavement is different. A lot depends on the circumstances of the death, the age of the person who has died, and our own individual emotional make-up. Some people want to tell the world how they feel and others button up, attempting to make life "business as usual."

But whatever our response, death challenges us. It's a shocking reminder of our own mortality and that of the people we love. It can make the world feel very unsafe and unleash many anxieties and fears. If we have faith it can be severely challenged: how could a God of love allow something so terrible to happen? On the other hand, some people believe that it is only their faith that enables them to keep going. Each of these responses is normal; there is no right or wrong way of grieving, of coming to terms with the death of someone we loved dearly.

This book was written in the early 1990s when the author worked in the BBC's religious broadcasting department. There, as series producer of the program "Living with Dying," she realized how much people drew strength from hearing how someone else lived through the experience of bereavement. Many viewers wrote in response to interviews featured in the program that dealt with bereavement.

This book is about sharing just a little of other people's experience of loss and hurt. No one person's experience is ever the same as another's—but by reading about how other people felt, and how they did or didn't cope, readers may find strength in knowing that they are not alone.

Introduction

The death of someone we love will be one of the most stressful and devastating events of our lives. Death is a shocking and bewildering experience and not something we can "get over" in a matter of weeks or months. Grief is a long and individual process, and no two persons' experience is ever identical.

The text of this book was written nearly ten years ago. But bereavement is timeless and the feelings that stem from loss are just as raw, no matter what the calendar year. One of the things that can help, however, is sharing the experience with someone who has been through a similar ordeal. And that is what this book offers—detailed stories of how other people felt, and came to live through, their bereavement. The feelings and thoughts expressed draw heavily on the real experiences of many bereaved people. Details and names have been changed, and narrative devices have been used. Each story captures different elements of bereavement that I have heard and read about, time after time. For, although each person's experience is unique, I believe there are common threads and hints of universal truths hidden within the process of grieving.

The wisdom and insights in these chapters came primarily from the many people I met and heard from in the course of my work on "Living with Dying". I am not, nor ever was, a bereavement counselor. But as a television producer my craft has been to listen to people who wish to share their experience and then to shape what I heard for a wider audience. In the course of the many years that I worked in religious programming, I met some remarkable people whose lives were devoted to working with the dying and the bereaved. People like Elisabeth Kübler-Ross who, at the time we met at her home in Virginia, was setting up a hospice for babies with the HIV virus and AIDS.

It is people like this who gave me a lasting insight into how much dying and death is an integral part of life, no matter how much we pretend it isn't. And it is the hundreds of viewers and listeners over the years who responded to programs about bereavement, or those who participated in interviews, who helped me to sense the roller-coaster experience of grief that can follow the death of someone who was dearly loved.

Sadly, in recent years there have been too many opportunities to see the emotional devastation caused to people after the sudden or untimely death of someone close to them. Should this book ever hint of "knowing it all" or offering seemingly easy answers, ignore them: there are times when there can be none. There are some situations when bereavement is painful beyond words and the lives of those who are left are changed, and scarred, forever. Their journey back to "normal" life is a long and hard one.

However, when I first wrote this book—and it's just as true today—I realized how ill-equipped we are as a society and as Christian communities to deal with bereavement. People will still try to avoid talking to someone who is newly bereaved. Many are frightened by the obvious pain and distress of someone who is grieving. Younger generations in particular have very little experience of death.

It's my hope that this book will enable bereaved people to draw strength from the experiences of others, and that anyone who wants to know more about the human condition of bereavement will feel better equipped the next time they're faced with a friend, colleague or relative who is grieving.

After ten years there are no individual people to thank—but this book could never have been written had my work not taken me to some of the dedicated people who work daily with the dying and the bereaved. They inspired me and helped me glimpse the eternal world which we so readily mask by the everyday. And I also acknowledge the immeasurable impact of the many people who, over the years, have written about their own experiences of bereavement to anonymous program-makers. In that honest and open sharing of experience, they shaped much of my thinking in this book.

Glasgow, January 2002

1

"So Alone!"
The Fact of Death

I am devastated at losing my husband, who was my best friend as well. Words cannot describe the loneliness and desolation I feel. We had been married for fifty-two years, and I feel like I've lost a part of myself.

I thought I was prepared for death, and for being on my own, but after thirty-five years of marriage, I don't think you ever can be "ready."

When everyone had gone home after the funeral, I felt incredibly lost and sad. I didn't know what I should do next. I quickly returned to work, but found I felt terribly tired and that the tears welled up all too easily. I felt guilty; I felt empty.

Death, no matter how it comes—whether expected or completely out of the blue—is an outrage. It can shake us to our very core and make us question the purpose of life itself. Why are we born, if only to die? Why love, if it only results in pain? How can someone be here one minute and irrevocably gone the next?

Death makes us question the meaning of life itself. It also stirs up all kinds of strong and overwhelming emotions: anger at the person who has died; resentment at the apparent unfairness of it all—"Why me? I've never done anyone any harm"; guilt at all the things that happened over the years which resulted in arguments; or guilt again at having taken that person for granted.

Yet death is inextricably a part of life. On an intellectual level we all know about death and say, wryly, "Well, the one certain thing about life is death." But on an emotional level, death appalls us. It takes from us people who are part of our lives, and it removes from us people that we love. We might have faith that we will see our loved ones again, or we might believe that we will never see them again. Either way we are left with a sense of uncertainty. And in the meantime, life goes on and somehow we need to learn to live without the person or people whom death has stolen from us.

The process of adapting to profound feelings of loss, of dealing with an overwhelming sensation of grief, and of beginning to live again is known as bereavement. The Oxford Dictionary defines the verb "bereave" as "rob, dispossess of, leave desolate," and these definitions aptly describe the responses felt by people coming to terms with the loss of someone they loved.

For people living in first-world nations, bereavement has become a particularly difficult process. In a developed, technological society, death itself has become a taboo subject. Advances in medical science, along with a huge general improvement in nutrition, hygiene and standards of living, have meant that, except through accident or rare illness, death has become a phenomenon of old age. It now somehow represents failure for the medical profession and is something the rest of us prefer not to think about and successfully manage to avoid.

These, of course, are sweeping generalizations, but society today is not accustomed to dealing with death on a regular basis. Although it is such a natural part of life, it really has become the extraordinary part. Fatal accidents attract lurid headlines in local and sometimes the national press: "Mother of two dies in crash." Death is also a convenient way of writing characters out of the ever-popular television "soaps." The result seems to be that the only contact many people have with death, for long periods in their own lives, is by means of the media or through make-believe.

Rather than make us more sympathetic to people who are recently bereaved, these changes seem to have the opposite effect. Many of those who are newly bereaved talk of people literally crossing the road to avoid talking to them. Some recall being asked, four or six weeks later, "Are you feeling better now?" They also say how much they need to talk about the person who has died, and yet how frequently that name is omitted from conversation.

Avoidance of talking about death (particularly our own) and confining it strictly to the world of drama or news headlines makes us ill-prepared to help the dying and the bereaved. When we also have to face the death of someone close to ourselves, we feel bewildered and confused.

Jane's story

Jane was thirty-two and working full time as a teacher at a local primary school. Her husband, John, was working long hours trying to build up his own business as a printer. For the past couple of years they had talked about starting a family but, with the rise in interest rates, the financial pressure on the business was great and they decided to wait until they were on a firmer financial footing. It was a Thursday evening, Jane recalls, when the phone rang. They had just finished a late meal and were watching television.

I picked up the phone from where I sat in my chair. My father said, "Jane," and then nothing else. He was breathing heavily and then began to cry. I remember shivering, and an icy flood of terror shot through my system. I was fearful about what he was trying to tell me. "Dad, what is it? Tell me!" Then, in a rush, he told me that my mom had collapsed at home late that afternoon and that he'd returned from work to find her lying on the living room floor. He'd called an ambulance, but she was dead by the time they got to the hospital.

I remember being unable to talk. John took the phone from me, talked to my dad, and soon we were driving the 200 miles to be with him. In one sense the days that followed are a complete blur, but I remember thinking, as we drove that night, that this wasn't real. It couldn't be happening to me. And yet one part of me must have known it was real, because I felt like the rug had been pulled out from under my feet and suddenly the world seemed like a very hostile place.

There are certain moments which still seem ingrained in my memory. Suddenly, when I'm doing something mundane like washing the dishes or driving home from work, one of those moments will just appear from nowhere and take me completely by surprise. It's difficult to get rid of, too; it's like I've got to keep going over and over it. One moment that keeps coming back is the day I started to go through my mother's things. I felt like an intruder working my way through her dresser drawers. These were her intimate things, and they reminded me—oh, so painfully—that there was a side to my mother I never knew. And as I feel that, I feel the guilt too. The accusing inner voice that says, "You shut your mother out; you didn't get to know her; you were too busy with your own life...." And so it goes on. I know too that she'd really have liked me to have had a baby, and I feel awful that I didn't have one because we had decided we couldn't afford it yet!

My mother's death was six months ago now, but I still feel devastated by it. I find it hard to believe she's really gone, and I keep thinking of things I want to tell her, things that I would never have talked to her about before. Suddenly, it's become important to me to have a child, but John says we still can't afford to. I'm worried about my dad, too. I'm terrified something's going to happen to him. I keep phoning him up to ask how he's doing, and find that I want to be with him more than I did.

You know, I hear myself say all these things.... I'm worried about this, terrified about that, guilty about the other, and I hardly recognize myself. I used to be so happy-go-lucky, but now that mom has died I suddenly feel very insecure. And although John's being really supportive, in a funny way I feel so lonely. My friends were all very considerate to begin with, but it's like they think I should be over it by now. None of them has lost a parent, and I think they find it uncomfortable to see how upset I still am.

❖❖❖

Grief, as Jane indicates, is a very lonely experience. The range of feelings—from hurt to anger, from jealousy to guilt, and also from love to feeling let down and abandoned by the person who died when you still needed him or her—can only be experienced by you. Other family members are learning to live with their own loss, but only you know how you are feeling at any one particular time. Even then, it's possible that you can't really identify what it is you are feeling. Your feelings may be confused and swing from one extreme to another.

People who are grieving can also experience a range of physical symptoms: insomnia, lack of appetite, headaches, and tiredness. Couple these with sadness and waves of unfamiliar and unpredictable feelings, and it is easy to see why this can be a very, very difficult time in anyone's life. We are so unprepared for it, in ourselves or in other people.

Christians in particular can find themselves thinking, *If only I had more faith in God, I wouldn't be feeling like this.* Yet for people who have a very strong faith, the pain can be just as great. Sometimes it can be worse.

Malcolm's story

Malcolm had been married to Julia for forty years. They led a normal life in a normal suburban neighborhood, and in the course of their marriage they faced very few ups and downs. One of their sadnesses was that they had never been able to have children, but that fact had brought them closer together and their marriage was a strong one.

Only a month after Malcolm's retirement, Julia was diagnosed with advanced lung cancer, and doctors announced that there was nothing further they could do. Throughout their married life Julia and Malcolm had attended church regularly and were regarded as stalwart parishioners. In the three months before her death Julia found more and more comfort in her faith; and the friendships she had formed in her church brought much support as people there flocked to help. Malcolm, though, felt his heart hardening. In prayer he pleaded with God to let Julia live, and when well-meaning friends spoke of God's mercy in allowing Julia a quick and dignified death, he felt an anger that he would never have expected.

Julia's death was dignified; her pain was well controlled and she received excellent nursing care at home. At her funeral service the church was packed, and the congregation sang out with full voice the hymns she had chosen, with gratitude for Julia's friendship. The presider spoke of Julia's calm and accepting faith, and of his certainty that she now was in a better place where she would know no more pain. Malcolm picks up the story from there.

I sat there in the church feeling cold and hard. I couldn't cry, but I felt overpowering anger. How could they be so cheerful about Julia's death; how dare they praise God for taking her away from me? All my life I had faithfully attended church, all my life I had believed in a God of love who heard us in our distress. Now I was doubting if any of it was really true. If it wasn't all a sham, and there really was a God, why had he not heard my prayers and let Julia live longer? I needed her.

The next few weeks I hid myself at home. I didn't want to see anyone, I certainly didn't want to talk. At first the people who had dropped by the house while Julia was ill came to visit. But because I was so reticent and distant they soon stopped coming. Father called a couple of times, but I was too ashamed to tell him that I now questioned whether or not there really was a God. So we just had a really stilted conversation that I think both of us found profoundly uncomfortable.

During this time I really let myself go. I didn't eat properly and I started to drink heavily. It was the only way I could get through the evening. The alcohol was like anesthesia that took my pain away because the loneliness I felt was unbearable.

I also couldn't believe deep down that Julia really had died. If I heard a noise I would think it was Julia—coming in from shopping or tidying things up in the bedroom—and then, a split second later, I'd have to tell myself again that no, it wasn't; Julia was dead.

I didn't wash my clothes, I didn't clean the house, and in my deepest moments of despair I'd find myself shouting at God, "Why did you take her?" Sometimes I'd whisper, "Come on, God—if you're really there, show me; prove it to me!" Julia had abandoned me by dying, and God had abandoned me too.

Then one afternoon, about two months after Julia's death, I just felt this tremendous surge of anger—at Julia for dying; at God for not being there; at our so-called friends who had quickly disappeared from the scene. I found myself picking up a table lamp made from heavy glass and hurling it with all of my strength through the living room window. It was like I had this desperate need to smash or destroy something; it had been bottled up for so long, and now it was erupting like a volcano. And then the tears came—virtually the first tears I had shed since Julia died—and I cried. How I cried! Heaving sobs that just went on and on...

I have no idea how much time passed, but suddenly I became aware that there was a police officer in the room. She was incredibly kind, explaining that the neighbors had alerted them because they had heard the sound of breaking glass. She made us some coffee and then sat with me, encouraging me to talk. And out it all came—all the stuff I've just told you, and lots more besides. Eventually, she said she had to go, but asked if she could contact a social worker. I wanted to say no, but by then I realized I probably needed some help to sort things out, so I agreed.

That was three years ago now, and I really thank God for that police officer. I only saw her that day, but through the social worker I eventually began attending a bereavement group. Everyone there had lost somebody close to them, and when we met we talked about how we were doing. It sounds morbid, but through that group I realized that I wasn't going crazy—even though you feel like it—and that other people felt like I did.

I still have my down moments, don't get me wrong, but gradually I've gotten myself together again. I'm not the same person I was before Julia's death; I never will be. But in a funny sort of way I'm stronger. Julia was always there for me, all the way through our married life, so I've had to learn to live on my own. I'm ashamed to say I've even had to learn how to cook. I'm pretty good at it now!

And my faith? It's back, quieter maybe, but much deeper. I realize God was there, all along. As the saying goes, if the sun is hidden by clouds it doesn't mean that it isn't there. I was so caught up in all that I was feeling, I just couldn't allow God to get close. But what I've also realized is that it was all right to get angry with God; maybe it's one of the few times I've truly been honest with the Lord. I'd always adopted my "Sunday-best" behavior before, but now I come to God as I really am. I realized that God could cope with my anger.

Grief comes in all shapes and sizes. Don't let anyone try and tell you how you should be feeling. And one thing's for sure—God will take all of it, just as it comes. I still miss Julia. A day doesn't go by that I don't think of her at least once. But I cherish some happy memories of our years together, and I really believe that one day we'll be together again.

◆◦◆◦◆

Malcolm's story is typical and indicates just how long the grieving journey and acceptance process can be. It also shows that grief can make us behave in ways that can take us by surprise and that we can find disturbing, even shaming. Losing someone we love to the finality of death turns our lives upside down. A void of longing and needing is opened up, and it takes time to adjust to that void. Whether we have a very strong faith or none at all, or are "somewhere in the middle," we will feel a void. God is not a replacement for human love. When we have lost someone who was a part of our life, someone who loved us and whom we loved in return, someone who cuddled us and held us and made us laugh, then we have a human right to miss that person.

Even if he or she was suffering and it came as a relief when the suffering ended, we will still mourn. We mourn for the very simple reason that a person we loved is no longer with us. And the right to mourn is one that nobody should try to take away from us and that we all need to learn to respect.

Obviously, there are degrees of "justice" in loss. The death of someone aged ninety, after a full and active life, has a sense of rightness to it. The death of a child of six, struck down by a drunken driver, seems tragic and outrageous. Both people will be mourned by those close to them, but while the first death can be accepted as "natural," the second will provoke anger and bitterness and will be a very difficult loss for the family to bear. Parents, grandparents, brothers and sisters will have a long way to travel before they feel that they have picked up the pieces of their lives again. In some cases marriages dissolve, so destructive is the grief felt by one or both parents.

So, where is God in all of this? Is God in the picture at all? Faith says that our God is at the very heart of the worst of our grieving. As the Scriptures tell us, God weeps with those who weep and yet also wipes away every tear. It is a reassuring and comforting image. But our humanity, our intellect, ask, "Just how is God a part of all this?" The words sound reassuring, the concept is desirable, but how do we know it's true?

Does it just boil down to faith after all? Perhaps through the experiences of others we can better see how God is an integral part of the lonely, aching grieving process.

Jennifer's story

Jennifer had just turned thirty when her life was turned horribly upside down. Two days into a family vacation at a popular Mediterranean resort, all seemed right with the world. Jennifer had lain back on the warm sand, feeling herself beginning to relax for the first time since her divorce had become final just three weeks before. Her two daughters, eight-year-old Emma and six-year-old Rosemary, were playing at the water's edge down on the beach. They were happily amusing themselves and seemed content to obey her instructions not to wander away on their own.

Jennifer nodded off into a light sleep and then, suddenly, found herself waking up, pangs of fear knotting her stomach. Where were the girls? They weren't at the water's edge any more. Terrified, not understanding where the fear was coming from but sensing that something was terribly wrong, she began to run the length of the beach to where a crowd of people had gathered at the bottom of a cliff. The drone of a helicopter could be heard overhead, and sirens were sounding in the distance. Then she saw Emma, sobbing, clutching a stranger's hand; and just a few yards away, at the bottom of the cliff, lay Rosemary's body. Jennifer's younger daughter was dead, her neck broken after a twenty-foot fall.

Four years afterward Jennifer shudders at the memory, remembering the struggle to retain her sanity.

I practiced my faith before Rosemary died. Although my marriage had ended in failure and some people at church seemed to disapprove of my divorce, my faith was strong and I had a real sense that God was somehow guiding my life.

So when Rosemary was killed by such a freak accident, I felt shattered. Perhaps I'd been wrong, and the God of love was really a cold punishing Being. Was Rosemary's death a punishment for my divorce? I just couldn't get the thought out of my head. It tormented me.

Friends arranged for me to spend a week-long retreat with a contemplative order. As the nuns chanted, their prayers echoed around the old chapel, and I sensed that God was very close. I felt a tangible presence of something holy, special, and welcoming. I realized that this was no "punishing" presence, but a loving one, just as I'd been taught and just as I had once believed. The tears poured down my face as, with gratitude, I praised God for his goodness.

How could I do it? My heart was still breaking over the loss of my daughter. The pain was still there, but I was able to see that God had not caused Rosemary to climb that cliff. Also, when I wondered why God hadn't eased her fall, I had to remember that the Father had not intervened when Jesus cried in agony from the cross, "My God, my God, why have you forsaken me?" I sensed a kind of natural law, or a God-given law, was at work. According to this law, we are born into life (and as infants in the womb we have no knowledge about what lies ahead); and when we die, whether young or old, we are born into the next world. Death is the "mechanism," the "vehicle," that takes our spirits on, like butterflies emerging from the chrysalis. I'm not saying that I believe God wanted Rosemary and caused her to fall; but her premature death—so awful by our standards—has ushered Rosemary into God's presence, and she's in very safe hands.

I have to believe this because, if there is no "next world" or heaven, then Rosemary's short life meant nothing. She was merely a random collection of cells that ceased to exist. But life just has to be more than that!

Jennifer's account of seeing God through the death of her daughter is remarkable. How right she is to look to the place of birth, life, and death in attempting to understand a tragic accident. Seeing that death is the means to "another phase" does lend value and meaning to this life. Although it will not take away the pain of grief, it does add meaning where one feels nothing but a sense of futility. Still experiencing the pain and the feelings of unfairness, Jennifer is the first to say that sometimes she cries out, "Why me? First a divorce and then my child's death!" But her faith lends a perspective that makes sense of it all.

So, is God really at the heart of our grief? Does God share in it? While welcoming another child into this new existence, does God also recognize those left behind who pay the price of human loving? It helped Jennifer to recall that Jesus, on the cross knew of the life to come but also felt the agony of being abandoned. It also helps to turn to John's account of the death of Lazarus, the brother of Martha and Mary.

The story of Lazarus is powerful. We read in chapter 11 of John's Gospel that Jesus loved Mary, Martha and Lazarus, but on hearing of Lazarus's illness, he waited two days before going to Bethany.

By the time Jesus and his disciples got to Bethany, Lazarus had already been dead for four days. According to the Jewish custom of the day, many people were there consoling the sisters. When Jesus arrived, both Martha and Mary rebuked him, asserting that if only he'd been present, he would have prevented Lazarus from dying. Mary and many of the other mourners were weeping, and Jesus, who had predicted that he would "wake Lazarus from sleep," wept too, being "deeply moved in spirit and troubled" (cf. Jn 11:33–35).

Although the Revised Standard Version of the Bible says Jesus was "greatly disturbed," the original Greek implies a sense of anger. Biblical commentators speculate why Jesus should feel such anger. Perhaps it was because his beloved friends had to endure such an ordeal? Just as we experience bereavement, Jesus too felt grief and frustration, both at the loss of a friend and at the pain Lazarus's sisters felt as they mourned their brother.

Jesus then raised Lazarus from the dead. Usually that is the focus of this particular story. But I want to emphasize that, even though Jesus knew Lazarus would live again, he was still so troubled by the weeping and distress of others that he, too, wept at the loss of his dear friend. Here we catch a glimpse of how God weeps with us in our grief, while at the same time knowing the reason for each death and having a greater purpose. The God who weeps with us and who shares our anger is also a God who is neither powerless nor impotent. Out of this tragedy can come re-creation and renewal.

In subsequent chapters we will be exploring some of the larger questions that death poses: What is the purpose of life? What is death? How do we learn more of the nature of God through all of this?

I also hope to explore practical, down-to-earth issues. The experiences of others who have lived through bereavement may be particularly valuable, and perhaps they can show us—as a society and as individuals—how we can better help those who grieve.

So Alone!

❖ Death is an outrage. Intellectually we may try to convince ourselves that death is merely part of the life cycle. When it comes close, however, it is shocking. We don't expect death. Its finality can be terrifying.

❖ Bereavement is a long process. We may not recover from it in days or weeks, much like a bad dose of flu. We need a long time to adjust to losing someone so important in our lives.

❖ Grief unlocks all kinds of strong feelings. Commonly people think they might be "going crazy," but bewildering feelings are perfectly normal. Another common feeling that surprises people is anger. One may feel anger at the loved one for daring to die, or even for something seemingly trivial, like failing to have cut the grass before "going out and getting killed!"

❖ Even if our faith is strong, we may still feel bereft. To lose someone we love leaves a void, and we need to acknowledge that loss. It's a price we pay for the gift of human love.

❖ Death is a natural part of life. Death allows our spirit to move on to the eternal life that, according to Church teaching, awaits us.

❖ God shares our grief. In the depth of the pain, the loss, the anger, and the confusion, God is right there with us.

2

Saying Goodbye
Acknowledging Reality

Once I knew that Matthew was dead, I asked the doctor if I could see him. I'm glad I did. It was only then, seeing his body at peace, that I finally grasped the reality of it all.

I talked with Dad about his funeral service about two weeks before he died. He chose two of the readings and the hymns. He made it clear that he wanted everyone who knew him to feel welcome. In lieu of flowers, he requested donations to cancer charities. It was a good service, and I was glad that he had planned it.

The service at the funeral home was so disappointing! We had to wait outside for the previous service to finish, and then the priest (who none of us knew) kept calling my deceased aunt Georgina, but we had always called her Jane. She hated being called Georgina; said it made her feel like she was a naughty schoolgirl! And then, for the hymns, we were singing along to a tape. So tacky!

Death has become a taboo subject in our world. Except for emergency service personnel, health professionals, ministers, and funeral directors, most of us meet death only through the television or newspapers. Many people claim that they have never even seen the body of someone who has died.

Today, however, psychologists and people who work in bereavement counseling assure us that seeing the body of a deceased loved one helps us to accept that person's death. Even if the death was the result of a car accident or another horrific event, it is usually possible to spend time with the body. If the medical staff feels that the deceased person's injuries are too great and too distressing, relatives and friends may sit beside the covered body, holding a hand or a ring.

Physical contact is recommended because the human mind is complex and sometimes confusing. When traumatic events happen to us, we subconsciously, and even consciously, find ways to deny them, particularly if we did not personally witness the event. As we face the reality of the trauma, painful as that can be, only then will we begin to find ways of dealing with it.

Death has become so alien to our everyday experience, so dreaded (if we're truly honest with ourselves), that it is very difficult to take in—especially if we were not present. Even if we were there, and know intellectually that someone has died, the heart can lag behind. Cords of love which knit our relationships with people we're close to are not severed by death. Taking time to be with the person who has just died provides an opportunity for the heart to catch up. And as reality sinks in, we begin to say goodbye.

Pauline's story

Pauline and her husband David had been married for sixteen years, and had children aged fourteen, eleven, and three. One evening David found that he had run out of his favorite tobacco. The convenience store two blocks away was open 24/7, so he decided to walk over. It was a pleasant evening and Pauline joined him. Their three-year-old was already asleep in bed and the other two children were busy doing homework, so Pauline felt safe leaving the house.

At the pedestrian crosswalk a van stopped for them. A car behind the van, however, failed to see the red light at the intersection and accelerated into the next lane past the van, hitting David as he was crossing the road. His body was dragged some distance and then fell back on the road. The driver stopped.

Pauline and a nurse who was walking by raced over to him. "Don't move him!" she ordered as Pauline cradled his head. The nurse felt David's pulse. "He's still alive, but he's very badly injured." After what felt like eternity but was only a matter of minutes, the police and an ambulance appeared. Pauline accompanied David in the ambulance, watching numbly.

I sat there, willing him to live. I'll never forget that journey. I kept praying that David would just open his eyes, but he never did. I just shook. My hands and legs wouldn't stop trembling. I watched the whole time as the paramedic treated David.

We raced up to the hospital, sirens blaring. The doors were flung open. Now I realize that my last glimpse of David alive was of him being taken away from me by a whole posse of white coats and uniforms. A nurse stopped me from following and ushered me into a waiting room. I don't know how long I sat there. All I remember is willing David to live. A police officer came, inquiring about the details of the accident. I can't remember if she or the nurse phoned my friend Anne to look after our children. A doctor arrived, saying that David needed emergency surgery. He had severe bleeding in his brain, and they had to relieve the pressure as soon as possible.

I just couldn't believe this was happening to me. It was all a nightmare. Soon, I would wake up. Ten o'clock. Just three hours since we'd decided to go for a walk. The door opened and time stood still. I'll never forget the look on the doctor's face. She put a hand on my shoulder and said, "I'm terribly sorry, but your husband died just a few minutes ago. He had extensive injuries. In time, he might have recovered, but the damage to the brain was too great."

I felt such pain, I just couldn't move from the chair. *No, not David, not us.* What had we done to deserve this? Then I began to laugh hysterically. All of this had happened because David wanted some tobacco. It was absurd. Who'd heard of anyone literally dying for a smoke!

21

And then the crying started. Deep, deep sobbing. More than anything else, I realized I desperately wanted to see David. I heard myself asking if I could see him. Surprisingly, I didn't think they'd let me, but they did. Then I got frightened, fearful of what he'd be like. Yet I really felt strongly that I wanted to go to him. He was my husband. Those white coats had whisked him away from me. I had to see him.

And I did, in a small room off the mortuary. Someone had asked if I wanted a chaplain, and he was there with me. He was very kind and asked me if I'd like him to pray. I did. I wanted to hear that David was committed into God's safe keeping. Then the chaplain encouraged me to sit with David while he remained quietly outside. All I remember is sitting beside David, stroking his face and, from time to time, kissing him. His head was covered in a bandage and there was a huge lump on his cheek. Otherwise he looked like he was sleeping.

I talked to him, told him how much I loved him. I asked him how on earth he thought I was going to manage without him. Then I got angry at him, furious that it was his smoking that had caused all this. Throughout it all, I kept expecting David to jump up and say, "Had you fooled there, didn't I?" Except, of course, he never did.

I returned the next day to see him after the autopsy. In a strange way I welcomed that, because it would show why he had died. This time I brought the children. I didn't really want them to come, but the two oldest kids had asked. I feared that they would be too impressed, but the chaplain had said it might help them. He stressed that the children should be given the choice without being forced one way or the other.

Anne kept the youngest outside while I went in with the other two. Jim, the eleven-year-old, touched his dad and remarked how cold he felt. I was surprised how different David looked now, compared to the previous night. His skin was almost waxy, and I had an overwhelming sense that this was the body David had left behind. The night before, David had looked as if he were asleep. Now it was like it was David, but it wasn't, all at the same time. Obviously we were all really upset, but we were able to cry together. We cuddled each other a lot, not talking very much. Then the boys left the room and Anne brought Janie in. She kept saying, "I want my Daddy," so I brought her over, saying gently, "Daddy died, Janie. He's gone to heaven to live with Jesus." And do you know what she said? It was the very question I was asking: "Why?"

How do you answer a question when you don't know the answer? All I could say was, "Janie, I don't know why. We all want Daddy here; but Jesus will take really good care of him."

Afterward I learned that some of David's family were shocked that I had taken the children, particularly Janie, to see him. But what's the best thing to do? Why not tell her that her daddy has died and let her see him lying peacefully? How could I just say that he's gone away? That he couldn't say goodbye? That she will never see him again? I'm convinced I did the right thing for her.

About two years after David's death I asked my sons if I had been wrong in letting them see their father's body. They assured me I wasn't. Jim even said he'd had these gruesome pictures in his mind of how his dad must have looked after being struck by a car. But after the viewing, the pictures had gone away.

I know that I needed to see David's body several times. I had to keep going back to check that he really was dead. I had dreaded seeing him after the autopsy, but he looked all right. At least I knew that no one could have saved him. The bleeding in his brain had done too much damage.

By the time it came to the funeral service I think I had accepted that David was dead. Certainly when the coffin slid away from view, I knew it was David's body and not David himself being lowered into the ground. That helped me enormously, otherwise I don't think I could ever have let them bury David. I loved him so much, but what was left was a shell that he no longer needed. Don't ask me where he was. I'm not sure what exactly happens after death, but I knew that what went to make David into the man I'd gladly have died for wasn't in that body any more.

◆◆◆◆

The journey to acceptance which the path of bereavement represents is a long and difficult process of learning to say goodbye. Goodbye means letting go. The separation is marked by sadness, it's true; but also by the realization that now things are different.

I don't know about you, but I've always hated good-byes. Many soaked tissues have marked my taking leave of people I'm close to—not because they have died, I might add, but because I'm saying goodbye.

Perhaps there is a parallel here. Departures are so painful for me because, apart from being sentimental at heart, I'm also feeling the separation from people I love. Bereavement is also about saying goodbye. Death is the great separator. It pushes someone we love from this world into the next life, and as the people left behind we have to learn to live with that separation. By saying goodbye, we acknowledge that the person we love has gone. The first stage is to allow ourselves to feel that loss.

That's so much easier to say than to do. So many things need to be done at the time of a death. Our busyness can keep the feelings at bay. Generally men have more difficulty expressing their loss. Women usually feel more free to cry in public than most men.

In this chapter "saying goodbye" takes two forms. First, it involves beginning to recognize the reality of the situation: death really has happened. Second, it means formalizing that goodbye in ritual: the funeral. People complete their goodbyes in various ways over a period of time. Later chapters will discuss long-term methods of parting.

Seeing the body, in death, is one way of recognizing the reality of what has happened. When death occurs in a hospital, most medical staff understand the benefits of loved ones seeing the body. But people should not feel forced to do so. It should be an individual decision.

Pauline instinctively asked to see her husband's body. What happens if there is no body or if the body is so severely damaged that it really would cause distress?

Alex's story

Alex's wife, Louise, died at the age of forty on a business trip to Hong Kong.

I never saw her body. She was cremated overseas and we only had a simple ceremony here. I was very calm through it all, and was back at work within a week. My colleagues kept saying things like, "You're so brave," and I was pleased that they thought I was coping well. Then a few days later Louise's suitcase, with all her personal effects, was returned to me. That did it. I broke down and sobbed. I realized that, in some way, I had still been expecting her to return. Now here was proof that she wouldn't. I think that's when I really started to grieve for her.

———————◆◈◆———————

Denial is a common human protective mechanism. At the beginning of serious illness, for example, symptoms are often ignored; the person hopes that they will go away. When they don't, and doctors begin to suggest that something serious might be going on, patients will often say, "I'm sure they're making a fuss about nothing." Or their friends and relatives will say, "It'll be fine, you'll see!" And when confirmation of serious illness does come, patients and families commonly wonder if the doctors have made a mistake or confused the results with another patient.

Later on the reverse may happen. Many people with a terminal illness know intuitively that they are dying, yet they feel compelled to continue the denial that others are living out around them.

It's easy to see why. Who wants to face the fact that we, or someone we love, might have cancer or any other life-threatening illness? Who wants to be reminded of the reality of mortality? These tragedies befall other people, not us.

That is why one of the most common initial reactions in bereavement is disbelief. We try to protect ourselves from our own mortality, and to protect the people we love. This is understandable, because living daily with such intense feeling is more than most people can bear. It is difficult to take in that it really has happened to us. Because of this, many people find that seeing the body of the person who has died is the first step in absorbing the truth of what has happened.

That was certainly Pauline's reaction when she spoke of her husband David's death. She said that it helped her separate David and all that she knew of him from the inert, battered body he had left behind. This seems to be a very common reaction. Whether or not they are religious, people often talk of sensing that the person they loved has left the body. They often say the body seems like an empty shell. This in turn can help in the process of saying goodbye and of letting go. It can be extremely distressing to think that the person we loved so dearly is about to be buried or cremated. Yet, being able to separate the body from the spirit means that when the coffin disappears from view, it is not the person as we knew him or her who is being buried, but the body that our loved one has no further need of.

The second step toward saying goodbye occurs through the ritual of the funeral. From the beginning of the human race some ceremony has marked the death of an individual. Egyptian pharaohs were buried with a collection of objects thought useful in the afterlife— drinking vessels, weapons, jewelry. Many societies set aside a ritual time of mourning, recognizing the need for grieving people to be given time to come to terms with their loss.

How did our society ever reduce the remembrance service marking someone's life and death to a twenty-minute stop at the funeral home followed by a few sandwiches and a drink? Retreating to comfortable ways and avoiding the pain which death brings— especially when unexpected or untimely—devalues the gift of life and denies the strength of human feeling and emotion. Of course, this kind of experience is not the only one that exists today. The rousing send-off represented by the wake can still be found; and other religious and cultural traditions do emphasize support for the people who are grieving and celebration of the life that has just passed.

Funerals are one way of showing how much we value a person's life. It is possible to add personal touches that comfort us and, later on, serve as a good memory. Not everyone will want to do this, feeling that the words already provided are all that they can take; but some people do become involved in the planning, and appreciate the opportunity.

Oliver and Naomi's story

Oliver and Naomi's life fell apart after their four-year-old son, Paul, was diagnosed with a rare and untreatable form of cancer. He was ill for just two months, spending most of that time in the hospital. Naomi virtually lived there so she could be with her son throughout the ordeal. She helped in his nursing, and the hospital staff became her friends. They were fond of Paul, as they were of all the children they nursed, but Paul was there for a comparatively long time and they grew to know him, learning how to engage his cooperation. During this time Oliver continued working; although he visited on weekends and during the evenings, he began to feel left out. There didn't seem to be anything he could do for Paul; Naomi and the staff were doing everything. He was just the breadwinner who showed up, bearing gifts of new toys or candy.

With Naomi sleeping at the hospital and spending so little time at home, Oliver grew increasingly lonely and isolated. There was no one he could talk with about it. His business colleagues were solicitous but anxious to avoid upsetting him by probing too deeply. Nearly all the people he knew in the neighborhood were really Naomi's friends.

It became apparent that Paul had very little time left. He slipped into unconsciousness, and Oliver took leave from work to join the vigil at Paul's bedside. He sat with Naomi, holding Paul's hand and stroking his hair, which had started to grow back after the chemotherapy.

They talked to him from time to time, cuddling him and holding him, but knew he could probably no longer hear. Occasionally they talked briefly to one another, mostly asking if the other was doing all right, yet aware that together they were holding a vigil of love as they watched their young son's life slip away.

From time to time members of the nursing and medical staff came to check on Paul, but everyone knew there was nothing further they could do. Now they cared for Oliver and Naomi, encouraging them to drink a little of this, eat a bite of that. These professionals who had become friends over the last weeks were not afraid to show their own sadness. They reached out to Oliver and Naomi, offering what little comfort they could—a hug here, a pat of the hand there.

The chaplain came too. He offered prayers for Paul and his parents and sat quietly with them until he was called away to meet the parents of a dangerously ill baby.

Paul died very peacefully at six that evening.

By eight, Oliver and Naomi were back in their home together. Naomi was tired and drained in a way Oliver had never seen before. He encouraged her to take one of the tranquilizers prescribed by a hospital doctor. With Naomi in bed asleep, Oliver began the task of phoning relatives and close friends to tell them that Paul had died.

It choked me to do it, but I realized that here was something I could do. During much of Paul's illness I had felt powerless. There had been so little I could do for him; now, though it was a grim role, there was something I could do. Naomi was completely exhausted, not surprisingly, so it was up to me.

When I phoned our pastor, who had been very good to us throughout Paul's illness, he asked if I would like to talk about the funeral service. I couldn't imagine what there was to discuss. I thought it was ashes to ashes, dust to dust, and all the other words the prayer books use. He said maybe there were other things we'd like to do. Suddenly I wanted to know more and asked if he could come over right away.

And he did, even though it was late by then. Father reviewed the service with me, and asked me to think about readings we might like. Were there particular hymns that Paul had enjoyed? Were there people who might like to read or offer the gifts at Mass? Suddenly my mind wandered. What was that chorus Paul always sang when he came back from religion class?

The pastor left me with a list of Scripture readings to look at, saying he would be in touch the next day. I sat down with the Bible. For the first time since my grandmother had given it to me, I opened it and worked my way through the readings. It was a little tricky to find them, but at least there was an index!

I sat there reading long after midnight. The words meant something in a way I had never noticed before. God hadn't really been a part of my life. Church was just a place for women and children. But in the silence of that house, where Paul's voice would never be heard again, I began to wonder.

Paul had died on a Thursday, and his funeral was the next Monday. Naomi, too, liked the idea of making Paul's service special. So on Friday morning we began to plan. Actually we enjoyed it. It was one last thing we could do for Paul, and something we could do together.

What did we do? Well, we opened it up to the entire neighborhood. A child's death is so sad, and we wanted whoever wanted to to come to the service, including children. We invited the hospital staff, my colleagues from work, as well as our relatives.

Paul's religion classmates had made an altar frontal with the words "Goodbye, Paul" on it. One of the doctors who had tried so hard to save Paul read 2 Corinthians 1:3-5; and I read the passage from Revelation 21 about the new heaven and the new earth. I wasn't sure I would be able to get through it, but I did. The last words were, "Those who conquer will inherit these things, and I will be their God and they will be my children." That verse said so much to Naomi and me when we had been trying to choose the readings; we both agreed that I should try to do it myself.

And the hymns? Well, the packed church all stood and sang, "Jesus Loves Me, This I Know," which was the chorus Paul had sung over and over again when he first learned it. One of the nurses from the hospital who has a beautiful voice had asked if she could sing at the service. We were delighted that she had asked, and she sang *"Pie Jesu"* from the *Fauré Requiem.*

I suspect everyone in the church was in tears at some point during the service, but that's all right. It was a service for Paul, and the beauty was that it felt like it. A few months later, one of my colleagues told me that he had enjoyed Paul's funeral. I knew exactly what he meant!

One of the blessings Naomi and I felt was the support of the people there—the neighbors, the hospital staff, our friends and relatives. And now you're going to think we really did go over the top, but we had some photos taken that day. The pastor said he didn't mind, so we had just a few taken. We've got them in an album now. The front simply says "Paul." We've put in it all of the pictures we believe tell the story of Paul's short life: the ultrasound picture when he was still a baby in the womb, pictures taken at his birth, his birthdays and holidays, and finally the funeral pictures. The very last photo is the one with the altar frontal saying, "Goodbye, Paul."

We really treasure that photo album. It's been three years now since Paul died and we don't look at it as much as we did in the early days. On the date of his birthday or the anniversary of his death, we will always spend time looking at it, remembering. And we have another child now, Emma, who is only six months old. When she's old enough, we'll tell her about Paul and let her share the memory of the brother she never knew.

When I tell people about Paul's funeral, they often ask me how I felt through it. Wasn't it too painful? But because Naomi and I were so well supported by others, and because everyone was sharing our grief that day, it was unexpectedly therapeutic. I cried, especially when I saw the altar piece. Perhaps if Paul had died suddenly I might have felt differently, but we had some time to adjust, and our grieving began on the day we were told he was terminally ill.

Oliver's moving account of Paul's funeral shows that it can be a good memory. Many people see the funeral service as something of an ordeal—largely because of the difficult emotions involved. Not everyone will feel that in similar circumstances they could have done the same as Oliver. But attending to such details for a loved one who has died can be a comforting way of paying our respects to or celebrating the person's life.

Saying goodbye

❖ Seeing is believing. Bereavement can be even more painful if there is a gap between our heads and our hearts. Intellectually we know that a death has occurred, but our hearts cannot accept it. Seeing the body of the person who died can help one begin to acknowledge the loss.

❖ Don't exclude children. Even very young children can be included. They sense that something is wrong; if they are excluded, they may feel that in some way the loss of the person was somehow their fault. Because they are confronted by violent death in television shows, we need to give them a chance to see that death can also be peaceful.

❖ Consider how to make the funeral a good memory for you and your family—a chance to say goodbye publicly and to commit your loved one to God's care. You can give the service a sense of the uniqueness of the life you are now mourning.

"It's Like My Heart Is Breaking!"
The Truth Sinks In

*Before Richard's funeral I was very busy. Making arrange-
ments, phoning friends and, would you believe, tidying the house?
But then afterward, it hit me—the sickening realization that
Richard was dead. He wasn't going to walk through the door,
grinning and saying, "Hey! I'll bet you thought I was gone for
good." The pain I felt then was almost physical. A deep, deep longing for Richard that nothing could touch.*

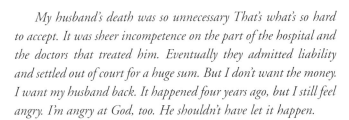

*After my mother died I had so many illnesses: colds, flu, any
bug that was going around. And I felt really tired too. It took so
much energy just to do the things I had to do that I didn't have
strength for anything else.*

*My husband's death was so unnecessary That's what's so hard
to accept. It was sheer incompetence on the part of the hospital and
the doctors that treated him. Eventually they admitted liability
and settled out of court for a huge sum. But I don't want the money.
I want my husband back. It happened four years ago, but I still feel
angry. I'm angry at God, too. He shouldn't have let it happen.*

Grief takes as many different forms as there are people who are grieving. Everyone's experience is unique, and there is no right or wrong way to get through it. There are, however, stages and reactions that are common to most people. For instance, grief can produce a strength of feeling that is unpredictable and can be frightening because of its sheer intensity. At other times it can create a disturbing absence of feeling—numbness and emptiness, a feeling of "deadness." Life becomes a routine of "going through the motions."

It is not particularly helpful to specify the stages of grieving according to a timescale. Most people go through a period of denial at the beginning. While it may last only a matter of hours for some, for others it may last months or even years. A lot depends on the circumstances of the death. Were we there? Was it expected? What was our relationship with the person? So much depends on our age, our beliefs, our personality and our life experience. All these affect the way we grieve.

Also, talking about stages of bereavement implies that there is a straightforward process where anger follows denial and depression follows anger. It isn't such a clear-cut process. People swing from phase to phase, even years later.

What is important is to grasp that there is no right or wrong way to grieve. There is no order in which we ought to feel certain emotions, and no timescale to follow. How we grieve is our own personal journey, which we have to make alone. There will be people and events along the way that may help us. There may be other grieving people who are sharing the same loss. But how we work out and live through our own grief is unique to each of us.

Normally, we draw strength from knowing that we are neither insane, nor odd, nor abnormal in the way we feel or think. We need to remember this when we grieve, especially if we feel we ought to be getting over it. Professionals who spend a lot of time with the bereaved say that it takes roughly two years for someone to work through a major bereavement. That's not to say that for two years we feel miserable and then suddenly we wake up one morning to find ourselves well again. It means that bereavement is a lengthy process. As time passes, the good spells will gradually grow longer; the feelings will become less intense, and the adaptation will get easier. But it is a process which takes time, and we proceed at our own pace.

Molly's story

Molly was sixty-two years old when her husband Mark died, three days after a severe heart attack.

I'm glad we had those three days. Mark was weak, but not in a lot of pain, and so we were able to talk together. The children and grandchildren were able to see him, and he was surrounded by so much love in those few days. From the moment our doctor sent him to the hospital, I just had the feeling that he would never leave there. And I was right. Mark had been making good progress, and then he'd had another heart attack. They tried to resuscitate him, but it was no good.

Our son took care of all the arrangements; in the months ahead, I was really grateful for his practical, down-to-earth help. He lives two hours away and he has his own life and family, but he made it clear that I could always phone if I needed something. I was so glad he said that, because I was clueless. I had never changed a light bulb before, or a plug; and I used to get in such a panic about how to pay bills. I didn't know anything about bank statements, direct debits, standing orders. Mark had looked after all of that.

But I've gotten ahead of myself. How did I feel in the first few days and weeks after Mark died? It's so difficult to say! I felt so many things: disbelief, anger, resentment, fear, sadness. To begin with, I fell apart. I cried and cried. How I ever got through the funeral I'll never know. I've always believed in God and received a lot of comfort from praying, but in the beginning, just after Mark had died, I couldn't pray at all. I was wrapped in a cocoon of grief and nothing could get through. I didn't have any words for what I felt. When my family and friends talked to me, although I answered, I couldn't really hear what they were saying.

I wasn't hungry. I wasn't thirsty. If somebody gave me something to eat or drink I'd take it, but I couldn't taste it. I found that I could fall asleep quite easily, but the dreams I had! Mark would be alive and well; we'd be planning things together, like a holiday or a house move. And then the plans would go wrong. I'd leave the passports or the tickets behind. Or I'd open the door of the new house and realize I didn't like it and wanted the old one back! These dreams were so vivid. I'd feel anxious and wake up suddenly. I'd reach across the bed to cuddle up to Mark and then be hit by the awful realization that he was dead. In the middle of the night, in the bed we'd shared for years, I would feel so alone, so desolate.

Nighttime is still the worst, three years later. There's nothing more lonely than waking up in the middle of the night and finding myself alone. It's the only time I feel scared in the house, and I really have to brace myself to get up and walk downstairs if I want something. But these are the times I now use for prayer. Not always. Sometimes I just want company and so I switch on the radio. Thank God for those people who work through the night. They have a real ministry, but I wonder if they see it that way.

It was about a month before I started to be able to do things around the house during the day. Even then, I would walk into a room to do something and then forget why I'd gone there. And the things I'd find in the fridge! One day I found a hairbrush that I had put there by mistake. All sorts of things would happen that would suddenly throw me into tears: mail which arrived for Mark, photographs I'd see when dusting, passing Mark's favorite chair.

My son and two daughters were so good. They were grieving too. We had tearful sessions together when we'd talk about things we'd done as a family, what Mark had said to them. I'd tell them about how we first met and how my mother didn't think that Mark was good enough for me. Of course, my children had their own responsibilities. It wasn't long before they had to go back to pick up their own lives. They all lived some distance away and couldn't just drop by, so there soon came a time when I was all on my own.

That first day, when I waved off the last of my children and shut the door behind me, I thought I'd die! The silence in the house was deafening. I didn't know what to do. I walked from room to room, touching things...straightening a cushion, smoothing a sheet. I put the radio on, then I switched it off a few minutes later. I tried to watch TV. I walked away, leaving the set on. I went into the garden, pulled up a few weeds, and then came back in again. I felt so aimless, so useless, and the day stretched ahead endlessly.

I could have gone out, but I was too scared. I didn't want to see people doing ordinary things, looking like they didn't have a care in the world. I found the noise of the traffic disturbing too. It felt aggressive, and I kept thinking it would get out of control and cars would swerve on to the pavement and knock me over.

So I stayed indoors. But by the middle of the afternoon I couldn't bear it any longer and phoned a friend to ask if she could come over. She stayed for a while. It helped, but then she had to leave, and the whole long evening loomed ahead.

By nine I could bear it no longer and went to bed. But sleep wouldn't come. I tossed and turned. I cried. I shouted at Mark, demanding to know why he'd left me like this. Then I became frightened that I was losing my mind. You shouldn't talk to the dead, I kept telling myself. It's not healthy! So, in the end I went downstairs and grabbed Mark's favorite bourbon, took it back to the bedroom, and drank two large glasses of the stuff. I hate whiskey normally, but that night, as it burned my throat every time I swallowed, it felt comforting.

There were lots of other days like that one. I realize now it's inevitable. You cannot possibly live with someone for forty-two years and not feel like you've had a limb amputated when they're gone. And, as a widowed friend of mine aptly puts it, it's like the limb was amputated without the benefit of anesthesia. Your whole lifestyle is affected too. I never eat at the table normally. I put the plate on my knee and watch television while I eat. I don't go out as much either. The friends who used to ask Mark and me over together don't ask me alone.

The worst thing still is the loneliness, even now. I've always lived with other people, and these last three years on my own have been awful. You can do a lot of things: go to church, do volunteer work, go to exercise classes, meet friends for coffee. But you can't do them every hour of the day. At some point you have to come back, shut the door behind you, and be on your own. That's when the loneliness can hit. Not always. I'm now at the stage when I can enjoy my own company for a short time, but the loneliness still gets to me sometimes.

I don't find it easy to say this. Women of my age are from a generation where you don't talk about sex, but I so miss being touched by someone who loves me. Mark and I were hardly the world's greatest lovers, but when we made love I felt so safe and so wanted. Now I'm on my own and sometimes I just long to be held. I see couples walking along the street hand in hand, or kissing one another, and a stab of jealousy runs through me that feels like real pain. Or I look in the mirror and I see the lines on my face, the ones which Mark used to tell me were lines of experience and character, and I just feel old and unfeminine.

I could be on my own for the next ten or twenty years. At the moment I feel useful because I can still get around and do things. I enjoy helping out as a volunteer at the local hospital, or going to stay with the children and keeping the grandchildren occupied. But there's going to come a day when age catches up and I won't have the same strength. I dread that, but it makes me think I've got to try to find ways of enjoying my own company more. It's not easy though.

◆◆◆◆◆

Bereavement is always an isolating experience to some degree, but the death of a partner almost always leads to the worst kind of loneliness. Sometimes it is overwhelming. After many years of marriage, of sharing so much of our lives with someone else, it is very difficult to get used to our own company. If we're younger and there are still children at home, then there will be other people around who need us. But if we are left to live on our own, there can be a real sense of uselessness. With the death of a partner it is likely that we not only mourn someone we loved dearly, but that we also grieve the loss of our previous way of life.

All this assumes a loving relationship. Not all partnerships are that positive. Sometimes death will usher in feelings of release and freedom. After thirty or so years of an unsatisfactory or even violent marriage, death is welcomed. In these circumstances perhaps the most difficult thing to handle is the guilt at feeling free.

Stages of Bereavement

Although people are individuals and mourn in different ways and at different times, there are recognized stages of grief. Not everyone will go through them all, but the following are the most common. They do not necessarily come in this order, and they often overlap.

Shock

The word shock is self-explanatory, and in bereavement its cause is obvious. What is not so obvious is how it manifests itself. It may be expressed as denial—not believing what has happened—or numbness, a lack of feeling, mechanically "going through the motions" during the events that follow a death. Sometimes it feels as if the carpet has been pulled from under our feet.

Shock also brings feelings that we normally associate with fear—butterflies in the stomach, loss of appetite, edginess. When we feel threatened or alarmed about something, our bodies release chemicals which are meant to help us to escape or fight an aggressor. Over the longer period of acute stress which bereavement brings, our bodies are subject to surges of adrenaline, making us feel panicky and breathless.

Other physical symptoms related to shock include insomnia, loss of appetite, loss of weight, headaches, heartburn, a susceptibility to infection, clumsiness and lack of concentration. Some may assimilate the symptoms of the person who has died.

Searching

When we lose something, we go searching for it. If a dog's owner goes away on vacation, the dog pines for its master. Pining in an animal is something we can recognize—a strength of feeling that is more than just missing the owner.

The searching stage of bereavement comes when we ourselves look for the person who has died, pining because he or she cannot be found. We pine out of loyalty and emotion, just as the dog does for the master who has gone away. Rationally we know that there is no point in searching. We know the person is dead, but emotionally there is still a desire to keep on looking.

This searching leads to imagining the face of "the lost one" in crowds or supermarkets or trains. Some people touch and feel the clothes of the person who has died because the smell or the memory brings them closer to the one they've lost. Quite often people will talk of "seeing" the dead person in the house, or "hearing" or even "smelling" the person. Such "glimpses" can be frightening, but they are a normal reaction to loss. Sometimes the searching is acted out with repeated visits to the cemetery, hoping to find the person again.

The restlessness many bereaved people feel springs from this need to search. We are less likely to say that we need to look for the person who has died. We probably don't even see it as such, but deep within us we feel we ought to be doing something; we just don't know what. It can be a preoccupying, all-consuming drive, if not a fully conscious one. No wonder there is little inclination left for food, work, sleep, or even other family members.

Anger

Anger and resentment are common. The anger comes because we need someone to blame for the loss we have sustained. The doctors may become the targets. We may blame ourselves—for something we did or did not do—the executor, the lawyer, the bank manager. It might even be the deceased—for "walking out on us"—or God for having "taken away" the person we loved.

So much of our adult life is about being in control—or struggling to be in control—of our own lives. All being well, the more mature we become, the more possible it is to build a secure environment for ourselves and those we love. Then along comes death and snatches someone we love. Not only do we want that person back and cannot have him or her, but we also lose a vital part of our security. The result is that the world around us now feels unsafe, and we feel a great sense of loss. We are outraged, angry.

The anger we feel is often taken out on others around us. Irritability, a tendency to flare up over small things, or pick quarrels are manifestations of the underlying anger. Sometimes it's a passive anger which never gets expressed but comes out by our being unkind or malicious.

Depression

Depression is the normal human reaction to loss. Bereavement is such a large loss that it is not surprising that feelings of depression or sadness can last a long time. The earlier stages of shock, searching and anger are initial reactions to a death. They occur because parts of us cannot yet believe or accept what has happened. Depression, however, comes when we accept the reality of the loss and react to it.

Depression may take the form of crying spells, fatigue, disturbed sleep rhythms, loss of interest in things around us, or loss of concentration. One person described it as the world losing color.

Despite the well-intentioned phrase "snap out of it," depression is not something that people can just shake off. It is a physical and mental condition which takes time to heal. Sometimes it needs professional help from doctors, counselors, or psychiatrists.

Resolution

This is the stage when we come to terms with, accept, and adapt to the loss we have sustained. A photograph or particular memory may still prompt pangs of grief, but we have good memories too and can enjoy them. Although we have not forgotten the person who died, we have lived and grown through the pain.

Knowing about these stages may be helpful in understanding the process of grief. It is so important to remember that it is a process which people go through in different ways and at different times. We cannot write off our searching phase and say, "Okay, the searching is over, now let's tackle anger."

Bereavement is not that tidy, because human reactions are complex. One thing is certain: if we were newly bereaved and went to sleep for two years, we wouldn't wake up and find ourself magically in the resolution stage having missed all the pain and messiness that the other stages entail! We would still have to face up to the loss and find ways of living with it. It's not time in itself that is the great healer, but the passing of time during which we have the opportunity to grieve and come through the ordeal.

James's story

James's story is a sad and realistic account of his journey through grief as he came to terms with his wife Christine's death. At the time of her death they were both in their early forties and had no children.

Christine had been out running early one evening. She came home, had a shower, and collapsed. That night she died in the hospital from a stroke. James asked that her organs be donated for transplant surgery.

On the outside I must have looked really in control. (They probably thought I was unfeeling.) But I'm used to taking charge and it just seemed to happen automatically. It was something to do, for heaven's sake! I phoned our pastor and he gave me the number of Christine's parents' parish. When I called there, the pastor agreed to go over and tell her parents in person. They are elderly and I didn't want them just to hear the news by phone.

That set the pattern for the next few days. I made myself really busy. Inside I kept getting these horrendous surges of feeling, as if I was really afraid about something, or nervous about giving the biggest and most important speech of my career. I couldn't sleep very much either. I kept going over what had happened. Time after time, my brain kept giving me the action replay, and it was impossible to hit the stop button.

Christine and I had been married for eight years. Before that I had lived on my own for over ten years, so being on my own in the house didn't worry me. In fact I didn't want people coming over, because they reminded me of why they were there and what had happened. At least when I was on my own I could "pretend" Christine wasn't dead and was just away for a few days.

It was strange the way I kept expecting her to walk through the door. Or I'd walk into the bathroom in the morning and be surprised that there wasn't a damp towel on the floor. (Christine always got to the shower before me, and I used to get really annoyed that she'd just leave the towel lying on the floor.) Who'd have thought that I'd actually miss tripping over it!

I found myself playing Christine's favorite CDs in the evening or just sitting and holding the silk dress that she'd had made when we visited Hong Kong for a short vacation. One night I even sprayed the pillow with that incredibly expensive perfume that she insisted on using every day. The smell of it, even now, reminds me of Christine.

For months I kept all of her things exactly where she'd left them. Her clothes hung in the wardrobe. Her make-up stayed in the bathroom. I couldn't bear to get rid of them. In fact, I needed them there, because to remove them would be like removing the last trace of Christine. I wasn't ready for that.

Was I angry? Oh, yes! There were times when I blamed Christine for "running away"—opting out of the human race. I know she didn't, there's no way she chose to die, but sometimes that's what I thought. Maybe if she hadn't been such an obsessive jogger she'd still be alive! All that running was a risk for somebody who already had a weak blood vessel. But then, she didn't know she had a time bomb sitting in her brain, so I can't really blame her!

Sometimes I would feel guilty that we were both so caught up in our careers that we didn't spend enough time together. If I had known we'd only be married for a short time, I'm sure things would have been different. We even might have decided to try to have children. It's funny, isn't it, how you hear of fatal accidents and illnesses happening to other people, but you never really think it might happen to you? I really thought we'd both live to be seventy or eighty!

Within two weeks of Christine's death I was back at work. I was desperate to get back, though I didn't know why. Now when I look back I can see that work at least was something familiar. The people hadn't changed, the job hadn't changed. In short, it was security. With

Christine gone, my whole life had been turned upside down, and work was the part of my life that was still the same. Perhaps I was running away too—running away from the terrible changes I faced at home.

It was terribly difficult to finish anything. I would start tasks and not finish them. When I was dictating letters I kept losing my place. I couldn't concentrate at all. Yet I would be the first one into the office in the morning and the last to leave at night. Deep down I suppose I didn't want to go home to face the emptiness there. And I was incredibly cranky, too! So many little things just seemed to set my nerves on edge: laughter in the office, things not going completely to plan, or even the phone ringing.

The guys in the office would invite me to join them for drinks after work, but I didn't want to go. On weekends I'd mope around the house, not wanting to do anything or go anywhere. I would sit mindlessly in front of the television, surfing channels. It was months before I was able to enjoy that time alone, and it was then that I found I was able to go back to church occasionally. But once there, I felt like a fish out of water. There were no other men my age there on their own, and I felt terribly conspicuous.

Then, just after Christmas (I can't talk about Christmas—it was too depressing. I've never felt so alone in my life!), the pastor asked if I'd host one of the lenten study groups. I was about to say no, like I did to everything else, when I found myself saying yes. On the first Thursday the group was to meet I made sure there was some decent coffee in the house and plenty of cookies. What a shock when I realized that it was the first time since Christine died that I had invited people to the house.

There were seven of us that night for a course on prayer. I'm certainly no expert, but then no one else was either (including the pastor, or so he said!). The discussion was honest and thought-provoking, and I found I actually enjoyed it. Besides, we were a very diverse group. There was a lovely couple in their seventies that I only knew by sight, a teenager and her friend from another church, and a professional couple who were new to the area. After everyone had gone, I realized that no one there had known Christine and I'd been able to relate to them as *me*.

That was an important discovery, because as the course continued, and ever after, I realized that I needed to build my own life, not mine and Christine's. I could never replace Christine, but I had to adapt to her not being around any more. At work that had been easy, because she had never been a part of that world. But outside work, it took me a good year or so to find things to fill the gap Christine had left behind.

◆◆◆

James's story reveals some of the key moments and issues in his journey through grief. By the end he is moving toward some kind of acceptance. It is also possible to get stuck on the way and to hit a point that you can't pass beyond. This was what Anna experienced.

Anna's story

Anna was sixteen when her mother died at age forty after a short illness. The family were members of a large church community, and the funeral for Anna's mother produced a packed church.

There was lots of singing, but the one thing I remember above everything else is the pastor's homily. He looked straight at me, caught my eye and said, "Don't mourn for your mother. She's gone to a much better place. God has called her home. Praise the Lord!" But I couldn't praise the Lord. I desperately wanted my mother back.

Every time I felt the tears beginning, for months afterward, I just remembered Father's words and prayed that God would forgive me for still missing my mother. Obviously I was a selfish Christian, because I could not be happy that my mother was in heaven! The time passed, slowly, as I tried to tame what I was feeling and not let it show. Over the years I got pretty good at it, too, except I kept the lid on so tightly I don't think I let myself feel anything.

Then, when I was about twenty, I was back at my dad's for a weekend. On Saturday afternoon a neighbor walked into our garden carrying Rosie, the cat that had been mine since she was a kitten. Rosie was dead, knocked down by a car, and our neighbor had found her lying in the road. I went crazy. Crying, sobbing—it just wouldn't stop. A doctor was called. I was given some pills and drifted off to sleep. But when I came to, I remembered Rosie, thought of mom and decided that life was all about death, so I might just as well get it over with. It seems I raided the medicine cabinet and swallowed whatever I could find—not that I remember much of that day. The next thing I recall was waking up in the hospital the next day.

Someone recommended that I see a psychiatrist. There were volunteers wandering around the hospital floor inviting people to the chapel for a service, so I found myself asking to speak to the chaplain instead. I still don't know why I was so insistent, but he came a few hours later and helped me so much. I told him all that had happened, and he very gently asked me if my picture of God had room for any love in it. I was about to say that of course it did, when an image rose in my mind of an authoritarian headmaster holding my mother against her will. It shook me, but instead of suppressing it as usual, I talked about it.

That was the beginning of a long journey back to life. At the advice of the psychiatrist and the chaplain I scheduled myself for therapy with a Christian psychologist who specialized in bereavement. My father was horrified, telling me that God had all the answers I'd ever need, but I persevered.

I'm so glad I did. I was able to see that faith or no faith, I had every right to grieve for my mother. I'd loved her, and it was normal to feel loss, separation, and grief. God didn't create us as he did, and Jesus didn't urge us to love one another with a quality love, only to deny our feelings of grief when death separates us. Grief is the price we pay for loving.

I also saw how, for the four years between mom's death and my breakdown, I had done little more than "exist." I'd used up so much energy just trying to deny my grief that there wasn't anything left. By denying my grief, I hadn't helped it go away. I had buried it deep inside. So when Rosie was killed, all that bottled-up, unexpressed grief just exploded.

Working with my therapist, I've faced the grief I felt over Mom's death. It wasn't easy and the pain is still there, but I had to express it in order to move on. And I have moved on. I enjoy life so much more. I've got more energy. I can look at my garden and see all the signs of new life around and truly praise God for all he has taught me, through my therapist and others. My faith is stronger and deeper, but now I recognize that as human beings we have our own lives to live—lives that are based on the here and now, with our hope in eternal life.

———————————◆◆◆◆———————————

Anna experienced being told that she shouldn't mourn, reflecting a particular Christian understanding. There are other people who, for various reasons, find they have never completed their grieving, sometimes years afterward. As in Anna's case, it may be the death of a pet, or some other loss (job layoff, illness, marriage break-up) that becomes the trigger to release pent-up grief. The reaction to the second loss might appear excessive and out of proportion, but this is because feelings that were blocked after the first loss are finally being released.

In other situations, the period of mourning may be going on indefinitely, with no resolution, following the bereavement. This can happen if the mourner had lived vicariously through the person who has since died—for example, a parent who attempts to live his or her desired life through the child. If that child dies tragically when young, there may be difficulty for a parent to move to acceptance, because the parent has lost his or her own "future" too. Or imagine a widow whose entire adult life had been bound up with her husband's.

If she had no independent life before his death, she may be unable to build a new life afterward because she is still grieving. Not only has she lost her husband, she has also lost her identity as "the husband's wife."

If you feel that you would like to talk with someone about the grief, anger, or depression that you still feel as the result of a death—no matter how long ago it happened—there are people you can approach. Ask your primary care physician or social service agency, or contact your diocese or parish for information about local bereavement services. Or you could contact a local hospice. Hospice workers offer services not only for their dying patients but also their relatives, before and after the death. They will be sympathetic to your wish to talk. Even if it is not possible for you to attend grief support meetings, the staff will be able to direct you to other organizations or a bereavement counselor.

At the end of the book you will find a list of organizations to contact for information, advice, or the chance to talk. Rather than offer professional counseling, they are available to "befriend" and listen. They can also offer the opportunity to meet other people who have suffered a similar loss. Don't be shy about getting in touch with others, because sometimes just talking to other people who feel like you do can make all the difference. You might also read Chapter 10, "Putting the Pieces Back Together Again," which describes how others have done just that.

"A Gift of Time"
Facing Terminal Illness

When my wife's illness was diagnosed as terminal cancer, she wanted to discuss the situation with me and the children. Afterward we did not dwell on the inevitable, but took each day as it came. She died about five weeks later. During that time we had discussed how I would manage without her, and I promised I would go to see the places we had planned to visit together.

Looking back, my only regret is that we never talked about what was happening to him. If we had talked then, maybe things would be easier now. I think that you must be told if somebody close to you has a terminal illness, because I feel that I was never really told this until two days before his death.

Through the hospice I have been encouraged to talk with the children about their father dying. Even though they do not want their father to die, they accept that his death would be a release from the pain and suffering he is enduring.

None of us knows when we are going to die. When someone is found to have a terminal illness, such news can be seen as a gift of time. A strange thought? Well, yes—initially. Yet, as the shock of the bad news lessens, the idea of a gift of time emerges. Instead of "if only," as is so often repeated in circumstances of sudden death *(if only I'd told him I loved him...if only I'd said I was sorry)*—a diagnosis of terminal illness offers a gift of real quality time: opportunities to talk, to share memories, to say things that need and want to be said. Knowing that death is only days, weeks, or months away can radically reduce the "if only" issues that remain.

That is the reason for this chapter on terminal illness in a book on bereavement. The process of "successful" bereavement is about finally letting go—letting go of all the things that tie you to the person who has died. It's not that you forget that you ever loved that person, but that you are able to treasure his or her love in a positive way. Sometimes it takes years, but in the crisis of learning that a loved one has a terminal illness beyond further medical intervention, the paradox of "a gift of time" can help people let go.

Mary's story

Mary was fifty-five years old and working full-time as a teacher when her husband, Sam, collapsed at home with severe chest pains. She immediately feared that he was having a heart attack and called the family doctor. The doctor disagreed: he believed Sam had a severe muscle strain that required rest. But Mary had been worried about Sam for weeks. He had lost weight and seemed very tired. She described this to the doctor and arranged for Sam to go to see a specialist at the local hospital.

X-rays revealed a shadow on one of the lungs and, two weeks later, Sam underwent a bronchoscopy—an examination which allows doctors to pass a tube into the lungs and see the cause of the shadow directly. The news was grim. Sam had advanced lung cancer and nothing further could be done for him medically.

Mary will never forget the day she found out. It was a beautiful spring day, with a clear blue sky and fresh green leaves on the trees—the kind of day when you feel glad to be alive. She and Sam were enjoying the warm sun in the garden when their family doctor called to tell them the news.

I was numb. I just could not take it in. Sam was ultra calm, asking the doctor matter-of-factly how long he had left; Sam didn't react when the doctor replied that nobody really knew. It could be as short as three months or as long as two years. Quite simply, the doctor said, the best thing was to take each day as it came and to make the most of it.

After the doctor left, we went indoors and sat on the sofa. We had left the patio doors open. The sounds of the world that had seemed so normal just a short time before washed over us as we sat there holding one another tightly. We cried, we kissed. Sam, who's not normally a romantic man, told me how much he loved me. I remember hearing the wind rustling in the trees outside and praying silently to God to give me the strength to get through all this, and to make things easy and pain-free for Sam.

◆◆◆◆◆

Sam and Mary were both actively involved in their local church and asked their pastor to visit them as soon as he could. He came that night, deeply upset. Sam and he had become friends, despite their heated differences about contemporary church music. They chatted, cried, and even laughed a little. Then the three of them prayed together, though not for long, because emotions were so raw and so confusing, it was hard to know what to pray for. They sat, heads bowed, with Mary and Sam holding hands as Father asked that God's presence be with them and that they be assured of God's love throughout the days and weeks ahead.

Mary said that it was difficult for her to sleep that night. As she lay there beside him, hearing the distant clock chiming the hours of the long, dark night, she cried silent tears, confused about why God had let this happen to them. Occasionally she reached out to stroke Sam's hair, unable to comprehend that at some short time in the future he wasn't going to be there any more.

I must have slept eventually, because I remember waking up feeling okay. Then, a split second later, this wave of sickening reality hit me. I should have gone to school that day but I called in sick. Two days later I was back at work and so was Sam.

Sometimes I found myself wondering if the doctors had confused the results. It was only two weeks before Sam was unable to work, and before my very eyes I could see him getting thinner and weaker. We cried a lot during the next few weeks: tears for ourselves and for a lot of "might-have-beens." I realized that Sam would never see any grandchildren we might have, and we'd been talking a lot about going on a grand tour around the world when he retired in a few years. That was obviously not going to happen now. I also thought of the plants and vegetables we had planted the day that the doctor called, and found myself crying because Sam would probably never see them full-grown. Ironically, he didn't really like gardening anyway.

But we had some good times too. We told the children the news right away. Although they were both living away from home, they came back to visit as often as they could. Friends from church and work came over often. Sometimes I wanted Sam to myself and resented the fact that he would put on a brave face for them. Then all I would be left with was an exhausted, sleepy husband. But he enjoyed their visits and I suppose I still got a lot of time with him, really.

Within six weeks, though, Sam became very weak and I took leave from work to be able to nurse him at home. A visiting nurse came every morning, and our family doctor was very good at visiting, too. Toward the end a hospice nurse came every evening as well.

Each day was precious to us, but we needed some kind of normality too. The television helped, providing a needed window to the outside world. Sometimes we just sat and talked, sharing memories about when we first met and some of the antics of the children when they were younger.

But Sam wanted to talk about the future as well. He made me promise that I wouldn't hang on to the house after he died unless I wanted it. He checked too that I knew about all the bills that were to be paid, the bank accounts, insurance policies, and his will.

We also talked about his funeral. Sam chose the hymns he wanted to be sung, and asked that a memorial tree be planted in his honor near Lake Windermere, because it was there that he had first felt deeply the presence of God.

During all this time together we became very close. We also found a great deal of comfort in prayer. A eucharistic minister would bring us communion once a week, and that was a very special time for all of us. I felt that it was helping hand Sam over into God's safekeeping, and we both always felt very peaceful afterward.

It was also a time of voyage. My grieving began the moment I knew that Sam had terminal cancer. During the weeks we had together, I was learning to say goodbye, beginning to let go of him. He was doing the same, preparing to face whatever lay ahead, because no matter how strong our faith, he had to move to the next stage alone and he also needed to learn to let go. As we learned to part from one another—I find it hard to describe, but there were moments that were really beautiful. We were completely honest with each other, without any pretense.

Sam stayed at home throughout his illness, thanks to wonderful local nursing support; but in the last few hours he slipped into a coma and I just sat beside him holding his hand. His breathing got very loud. There were long gaps between each breath, but he was very peaceful. I thought I would be frightened, but I wasn't. Then Sam took one last deep breath. Almost like a whisper, the breath was released, and all the muscles of his face relaxed. I realized Sam had gone. Very quietly. Very gently.

The children were with him at the very end; they both had said they wanted to be there. They'd been back with us for a couple of days, and when the nursing staff told us they thought Sam's death would be very soon, we took turns to sit with him. But at the moment when he died we were all there, and I was so glad that we were all together. It was such an intimate moment— one that I don't think any of us will ever forget. It was also a very peaceful death, and I think it helped us all to see that death doesn't need to be frightening.

By the time Sam died, I think I was ready for his death. I was appalled by how ravaged his body had become, his need for powerful pain relief, and the forced indignity of being unable to care for himself. My strong, supportive other half—whom I'd always relied on to be there—was now completely dependent, and that's very hard to deal with. Although I've talked about how close we became during his illness, I don't want to disguise how revolting it can also be. At times I felt revulsion at what the cancer had done to his body. Sam felt that too. We didn't talk about it much, but we were honest about it when we did, and then quickly moved on to talk about other things.

Although it was dreadful to see Sam's body literally wasting before my eyes, I'm selfishly grateful that he died this way. Whenever I read of people who've lost loved ones through sudden death, I can sense the enormous shock and disbelief they must feel. But I know that Sam was ready for death when it came. It was a release, and the weeks that led to it gave us a chance to share so much, and to learn to part. Also I'm grateful that Sam was able to help me practically. I had always left financial matters to him, but he made sure I knew how to sort out the life insurance, and helped me see what I'd need to do after his death. At the time I'd rather not have discussed it—it seemed insensitive, but he was right to force me to think about it all, because (as he rightly guessed) I wouldn't have had a clue!

◆◆◆◆

Mary's experience of her husband's death was a good one—if an experience of death could ever be called good. She can look back on their time together with very few regrets. The closeness and intimacy of those last few weeks are a very precious memory for her, and she was very grateful that she was able to care for Sam at home right up to his death.

Obviously I grieved for Sam after his death. There were some long, lonely, and painful times. Even now, three years later, I still miss him. I catch myself wondering what Sam would have thought about something that's happened.

I know that having that time together really helped me get through this bereavement. Most important was that we were able to talk in a way that we really hadn't before. Our love was very strong when he died. If the whole depressing experience of seeing a loved one die means anything at all, it means experiencing a very special and pure quality of human loving—not just between Sam and me, but with the children and with all our friends who were there all the way through: cooking meals, bringing books, finding ways to let us know that we were not forgotten. I think that's how I know God was with us through it all—in that very special quality of loving that the children and I experienced. Selfish though it might seem, I do thank God that we had what truly was a gift of time.

———◆◆◆◆◆———

One significant development in terminal illness during the last century has been the hospice movement. Hospices are the result of scientific breakthroughs in the treatment of disease and the consequent longer life expectancy in many First World countries. Because of hospice care, death does not need to represent defeat, and dying people do not need to be forgotten.

One of the pioneers of the hospice movement was Elisabeth Kübler-Ross, a remarkable woman who believed passionately that society should recognize death as part of life. She was the first to use the phrase "dealing with the unfinished business."

Although this phrase sounds like sociological jargon that makes us cringe, it represents a crucial opportunity offered by terminal illness. The time that remains can become an opportunity for a person to sort things out—emotionally as well as practically.

On an emotional level, it may mean talking about embarrassing or shameful things that never had been discussed before. Incidents that happened years ago may have bred resentment and bad will ever since. It may be a time to ask or seek forgiveness for broken relationships, spiteful jealousies, even for abuse—sexual, mental, or physical. It is also a time to express what probably goes unsaid much of the time: that people in our lives are loved just as they are.

On the practical level, "dealing with the unfinished business" may mean sorting out what should become of the home, drawing up a will which reflects the wishes of the person who is soon to die, or even planning the funeral service.

We also have to anticipate some of the smaller details. The reality today is that dealing with the death of someone close to us brings with it bureaucracy, procedures, and paper work—all when we are least able to think rationally about any of it. The kinds of contacts we need to make after a death are not just with relatives and friends, doctors, funeral directors, and clergy; we also need to deal with banks, real estate agents, insurance companies, lawyers, electricity and gas and telephone companies, and the list goes on.

These details may sound trivial, and in some ways they are; but with the advanced warning offered by terminal illness, at least there is an opportunity to locate important documents. Calculating though it seems, the administrative tasks surrounding death can happen more smoothly. The days ahead will be traumatic enough without the added burden of legal disputes and wranglings.

Lastly, while the "unfinished business" concerns practical and emotional matters, it is even more about spiritual considerations.

Until recently people used to debate whether those with a terminal illness should be informed. Now there is a greater acceptance that the patient and the relatives ought to know. Those who work with the dying say that patients intuitively sense they will die soon, even if nothing has been told them. When everyone knows the severity of a loved one's condition, choices can be made about how best to use the remaining time.

This time will be an emotional and spiritual roller-coaster, whether it is days, weeks, or months. In the early days there will be a lot of disbelief: "The doctors gave me the wrong results.... It's not as bad as they think." In between there will be moments of immense anguish and bleakness, and cries of "Why me, God? Why now?" (This, of course, is a generalization. If we could learn just one thing about bereavement and grief, it is that everyone's experience is unique. There is no right or wrong way to grieve, no typical pattern to follow.)

But in terminal illness, the time is there for everyone involved. For the person of faith, or the person who simply feels that now is the moment finally to confront the spiritual nature of life, it can be "extra time" to turn to God and, if necessary, make things right.

In some Christian churches, sacramental confession and absolution are a normal part of faith life; others do not have the practice. Common to all is the understanding that human beings are not perfect creatures—that the life, death, and resurrection of Jesus opened up a new relationship with God. So this gift of time, regardless of the person's standing before the illness, is an opportunity to reconcile with God and with other people.

It may be important to ask God's forgiveness for a particular relationship that has been destructive and unloving: perhaps a child left home after a serious quarrel and has remained distant ever since. It may be less dramatic: perhaps a relationship just might have been different. It is a cliché to say that the clock can never be turned back. Of course it can't. But the time that is left can still be used to improve matters. Asking forgiveness of God is one thing, but it may also involve getting in touch with the person who has suffered much heartache and bad feeling and asking that person's forgiveness too.

In a spiritual sense this gift of time may open one up to God in a way that has never happened before. Even people who have attended church services Sunday in, Sunday out, year in, year out, may find their faith completely rocked by the news that a loved one will die shortly. God can become a habit rather than a challenge. It may take something earth-shattering to force us to realize what we believe deep down.

It may become a frightening time, because we may suddenly find that our faith isn't as strong as we thought. Or we may get angry at God for letting this happen, or doubt whether God is even there, or think that God has in some way wished this on us because we haven't been good enough. These are all perfectly legitimate reactions. Where loss is concerned, there are no right or wrong feelings or beliefs. We feel what we feel and we believe what we believe; and these feelings and beliefs can change from day to day, even hour to hour.

The important, steadying factor in all of this is God's rock-like and continuous love for us, no matter how desperate and weak we feel. It is love which is freely offered and freely given, and it comes because God also shares the pain and the anguish that are an inseparable part of loving.

In all our anguish, we can become closer to God than we have ever been before. Imminent death focuses our minds on the essential elements of life. Suddenly things pale into insignificance that used to seem so important, such as where to go on vacation or the fact that the next-door neighbor keeps parking her car in front of our house. Instead, the things that are spotlighted are those parts of life that we know we are going to miss like crazy: friends, relatives, country walks on clear autumn days, laughter, love, and all those things that make it so good to be alive. Life, with all its ups and downs, seems a very precious gift, and with that sense of preciousness comes a deep, deep appreciation of the Giver, the Creator of it all.

While we may value the spiritual present, we may also anticipate the spiritual future. What is life after death going to be like? Just as we had no notion before we were born of what life beyond the womb would be like, so we can barely imagine anything new after death. We simply have to trust that it is better and closer to the absolute Love that created us and called our world into being.

At this point, it probably won't mean a lot to use classical theological words such as heaven, salvation, and eternal glory. If we want to, of course, each of us can read the Old and New Testaments and ask God to show us, even to reassure us, about what life means and what is in store for us beyond the grave. But a better aim would be to search for complete honesty, with each other and with God. It's a time to search with an urgency we may never have known before. And it's also a time to grow into the closer presence of God which normal life doesn't always permit.

Linda's story

Linda was in her mid-twenties when her mother was diagnosed with motor neurone disease, a horrific, paralyzing disease of the nervous system.

She wasn't too bad in the beginning; in fact, she looked fine to me. I tried to forget that she was ill and to get on with my own life. I've always been terrified of illness and hospitals, but I didn't realize how debilitating the disease could be. Then, too, I suppose I just didn't want to face up to the fact that Mom would die soon.

I realized I was finding excuses for not going over to see her, and I dreaded answering the phone in case she was calling. Inside I felt guilty about this, but I also felt angry with her that she had gone and contracted the disease. Then, one day, my boyfriend challenged me. He called me some things that really hurt, and we had a huge fight. He told me that his father had died in an accident at work, and that to this day he felt awful that they'd had words the last time he had seen his dad alive.

I hated Jimmy then for what he said to me, but once my temper cooled I realized the truth of what he said. The next evening I went to Mom's and for the first time could see how she must be feeling—facing a grave illness, divorced, and her only child finding all kinds of reasons not to visit.

We began to talk. She told me a lot about her childhood and early days of marriage that I never knew. Then she talked about her death and of how frightened she felt. I didn't know what to say. In the end all I could do was fling my arms around her, and we cried together.

Over the next two years Mom became more and more disabled. For some time I moved in with her, but she soon needed more nursing care than I could give. Then she started to talk about suicide and euthanasia. The suggestion horrified me. I sensed her fear of what might lay ahead—losing her speech, being unable to swallow—and I began to understand her desperation. I made her promise to call me when she was feeling overwhelmed. Even so, whenever I came in at night I dreaded finding that she'd gone ahead and ended her own life.

By now I also faced a decision about how best to care for Mom. I was already taking time off from work, and although my employers were sympathetic, I couldn't imagine the arrangement lasting very long. The choices seemed to be to either give up work altogether, or admit Mom into a decent nursing home. We talked about it. She said that she didn't want me to ruin my career for her, and besides, she'd feel more comfortable in a home.

The first time I had to leave her in that home I felt such enormous guilt. What sort of daughter was I to put my career before my mother? The staff there all assured me that I was doing the right thing. When I went to bed that night I realized that I wouldn't have to get up to help Mom to the bathroom, and I felt such relief. But with the relief, the guilt came back.

Mom hated that home. For a week she kept putting on a brave face, but then one day I dropped by at lunchtime and found her all stressed out. She told me that she wanted to come home, or else to die. It felt like blackmail, and while I can't say I hated her for doing it to me, I wasn't far from hate. I just didn't know what to do. I knew I couldn't cope with her at home, but I couldn't bear to see her so desperate. It wasn't that I didn't love her. She just needed more care than I'd be able to give.

Mom contracted pneumonia and died a month later. I don't think she ever forgave me for not taking her home. When I visited during those last weeks, the happy relationship we had before became strained. She would look at me with dark, piercing eyes, and I felt she was judging me and finding me wanting. So many people have told me I did the right thing, but it spoiled those last days together.

We had shared so much before then, but in the end it was like one of those awkward goodbyes at railway stations, wanting the train to leave so you don't have to struggle with small talk to cover the discomfort. And then as soon as the train leaves, you remember things that you meant to say.

Linda knows there were no other options for her, but still has enormous sadness that she and her mother were never reconciled.

Deep down I'm grateful that when Mom first became ill I came to know her as a person more than a mother, if you know what I mean. I recognize that toward the end neither of us could quite face up to the parting. For Mom, going home meant turning the clock back and getting better. For me that time in the nursing home allowed me to distance myself from her distressing illness. I wish that she could have died content, and I know she wasn't. One part of her was ready to die because she hated being so disabled, but the other still wanted to live. And even if I had that time over again, I don't know how I could have made it any different.

<hr>

Linda experienced the gift of time with ambivalence. She was able to draw closer to her mother, but she regretted that her mother's last few weeks seemed so unhappy. One of the dangers of speaking almost romantically about the gift of time is that false expectations may arise—practical, emotional, and spiritual.

Nevertheless, this is time that we can spend as we wish, and as we feel, with the person who is dying. The last days together may be a remarkable time of emotional and spiritual sharing, though they may also be marred by pain or partially unresolved anger and resentment. It may be that we long so much for a loved one's suffering to end that we pray for death to come soon. To do so is not to reject the gift of time, for it is also a loving response to want to see an end to the person's suffering.

The question is whether the last days of the dying person could have been better than they were. But we need to avoid wishful thinking. Deaths such as these are tough. Just because someone is dying, it doesn't necessarily mean the person becomes saintly and sweet; people generally retain the distinctive weaknesses and strengths for which they have been loved. Arrangements for nursing care need to be appropriate and realistic, as does the amount of care we can give ourselves. What we can do depends on so many factors. We must be open to give and to listen without impossible goals, respecting the pace so that the dying person does not become resentful. It is better to be sensitive to the person's wishes, and to speak of our love for him or her.

The gift of time is different for everyone. One young woman who was dying from leukemia wrote a "Letter to the Living," which she asked her brother to read aloud at her funeral. It was a remarkable letter and began with the words that follow, included here as a fitting way to end this chapter.

As the prospect of dying grows closer I am constantly wondering what it holds in store for me. I choose to believe that it will not be an ending but a transition from one state to another, from a physical reality to a spiritual one. Twenty years ago I purchased my ticket for this life; now the time has come to hand it back and move on to new challenges and new joys. Death holds no terror for me.

"I Never Even Said Goodbye"
Sudden Death

It was almost midnight when the doorbell rang. Two police officers were there. "Mrs. Green?" I nodded. "Can we come in?" They were ill at ease and I suddenly felt very cold. "It's bad news, I'm afraid. We have reason to believe your husband was killed in a pile-up on the highway late this evening." No, it couldn't be. I'd only spoken to him on the phone at six. There had to be some mistake. But there wasn't!

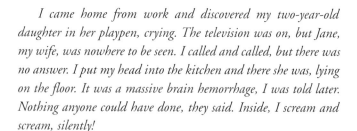

I came home from work and discovered my two-year-old daughter in her playpen, crying. The television was on, but Jane, my wife, was nowhere to be seen. I called and called, but there was no answer. I put my head into the kitchen and there she was, lying on the floor. It was a massive brain hemorrhage, I was told later. Nothing anyone could have done, they said. Inside, I scream and scream, silently!

Our son Jacob went to the hospital for a routine operation. Next thing I knew he was in intensive care on life-support. Two long days and nights we sat there, willing him to live, but there was no hope. We donated his organs because he'd have wanted us to do that. He would have been eighteen next week.

I've often heard people say, "When my number's up, I want to go suddenly. Here one minute, gone the next!" The thought has certain attractions: no pain, no worry, no time to think about what we might miss. For the people left behind, however, the shock is enormous. When we wave goodbye to a perfectly healthy person and only hours later hear of that person's death, it is very difficult to believe. Suddenly we are thrown into a world of autopsies, investigations, coroners, registrars, and funeral directors. Not only is there no warning of the death, no time to adjust or begin to prepare, but a sudden or accidental death has to be shared—not just with the others who mourn, but with the legal world as well.

In the midst of what is probably the most shocking event we have ever encountered, the law requires in certain circumstances that a medical certificate of the cause of death cannot be issued. In these instances, deaths must be reported to a coroner. For many of us the word "coroner" belongs to the world of TV fiction, because it is often the first point of contact in a detective story where foul play is suspected. So to hear that a certificate of cause of death cannot be issued until a coroner has been consulted is, at best, alarming, and at worst terrifying.

The involvement of the coroner may just be a formality, but it is the coroner's decision whether or not an autopsy or an investigation is necessary. It is not the coroner's job to determine civil or criminal liabilities, but to establish the cause of death. If the death was sudden, inexplicable or suspicious, the case may be referred to a medical examiner who has the option of performing the autopsy. Only when the coroner is satisfied about the cause of death can a death certificate be issued.

Just noting the legal terminology feels forbidding. No wonder relatives can feel completely lost at a time when they are already in deep shock.

Joan's story

Joan was going through this kind of living nightmare. She was twenty-nine and had just moved 200 miles north to be with her husband who was starting a new job. They had recently moved into a new home with a large mortgage and had invested virtually all of their savings into new furniture, curtains, and carpets. It felt like the dream home they had always wanted. They had agreed that Joan would wait a few months before finding herself a job locally, so that she could get to know the area and make the new house feel like home.

Two months after we moved in, Chris came home from work with a splitting headache and a really sore back. One of his colleagues from work was coming for dinner that night. Chris wanted me to meet new people, so he was reluctant to call it off. Instead he took some painkillers and soon began to feel better.

The dinner went well, though Chris didn't eat very much. He drank quite a lot of wine, joking that it was purely medicinal. By bedtime he looked wrung out and was running a temperature, but said he would just take some more painkillers and be back in shape by tomorrow. In bed I cuddled up to him, kissed him, and thanked him for helping me meet new people.

Those turned out to be the last words I spoke to him. The next morning I found him dead beside me. Even now, four years later, I can't describe what I felt or even what I did. I'm told I dialed 911, but I don't even remember doing that.

Chris's parents and my mom and dad came to stay with me. It was awful, just awful. There was an autopsy to see why he had died, and then I was asked questions about how much he'd drunk and how many pills he'd taken. Had he been upset? Was he worried about anything? Then it clicked. They wanted to know if my husband had taken his own life. No, he didn't, I screamed at them.

I couldn't understand why they wouldn't let us hold the funeral. I just wanted to get away from it all. Then, after all sorts of tests (I shudder every time I think of them cutting Chris's body into pieces), they said he had died from a rare but virulent virus. The alcohol and the painkillers had been contributing factors, or something like that.

The whole thing became even more of a nightmare. Chris hadn't left a will, he had said there was plenty of time for that! There was a problem with the life insurance and they said they wouldn't pay, so I'd either have to make the mortgage payments or the house would be repossessed. The car was taken back by his company. Chris's family blamed me for his death, and one of his sisters started sending me hate mail. It was all too much for me. A doctor put me on to tranquilizers and sleeping pills, and if it hadn't been for my parents I think I would just have swallowed the whole bottle and gone to join Chris.

Eventually, the insurance firm changed its mind, but by then the house was nearly sold anyway. I hated it. The brand new things I'd really wanted in our new home just mocked me.

One year later, I was a wealthy zombie living with my parents. I had no friends; I didn't want to go out. I lived on pills to stop me from feeling and pills to make me sleep. My parents were at their wits end. I couldn't cry, I couldn't concentrate on anything for more than a few minutes, and I could sit in the same chair for hours just gazing out of the window.

Then one day Mom came into my bedroom and said she had arranged for me to go and see a counselor. I just nodded. I'd agree to anything just to be left in peace. Two days later I went to the counselor and began what I now see was my first step back to life.

It took a long, long time. I'd become addicted to prescription drugs, and kicking that habit was bad enough. But over the months that followed I began the painful journey to where I am now. I began to express the grief that I'd bottled up for so long. I wrote a letter to Chris, telling him how angry I was at what he'd done to me, and read it out loud to the counselor. By the end I was crying, whispering, "But I loved you."

An old school friend began stopping by my parents' house. She'd just gotten a divorce and was still on edge, so we made quite a pair. We would go out for a drink or a walk, and one night we even attempted a movie. Ever so gradually, I began to come around. I started a part-time job at a day center for people with learning disabilities. They taught me so much. It was like they could feel how much I still hurt and gave me so much love.

On the second anniversary of Chris's death I went by myself to the cemetery where he was buried—the first time I'd been there since Chris had died. It was the city we met in and where Chris's parents still lived. I just sat at the graveside, cried a lot, and then started talking aloud to Chris, telling him what I was doing and how sorry I was that I hadn't stopped him from taking all those pills. At some point I realized that two people were standing close by. Our eyes met and then slowly they walked toward me. I cried again and just walked into their arms. It was Chris's parents, and we just stood there for ages holding each other, not saying a word.

Then the apologies started. Me—for not having been in touch. Them—for blaming me. It was like a scene from a tear-jerker, but it was real. I went back to their house and talked for hours about Chris. I told them things they'd never heard before. They told me about his childhood and how proud they had been when he had landed such a good job in the north. "What a waste!" his dad said. And it was.

Those words played over and over in my head on the way back home. With a shock I realized I had wasted a lot of my own life over the last two years. I was struck by how fragile life was, and made a late New Year's resolution that no matter how little or how much of life there was ahead of me, I was going to live it! To the surprise of my parents I got home and took them out for dinner to the most expensive restaurant in town—just a small "thank you" for the way they had stood by me.

For Joan the sudden death of her husband was even more of a shock because they were young, and because they had never even considered the possibility of death. That isn't always the case.

Gerald's story

Sylvia and Gerald had been married for thirty-nine years and had a number of what they used to term "near misses." Gerald had been seriously injured in a car accident; Sylvia had been successfully treated for cancer. Theirs was a fiery relationship, even after all the time they had spent together. It didn't take much for one or the other to start arguing if something wasn't quite right.

One April day was "one of those days." It was breakfast time and Gerald was annoyed because none of his usual breakfast cereal was left. He exploded and went stomping off to his workshop in the garden.

At about eleven I ventured out to make up, but there was no sign of Sylvia. Her coat and handbag were gone, so I assumed she had gone shopping. I made coffee and settled down to read the newspaper. By lunchtime there was still no sign of her, and I began to feel uneasy. She wouldn't have walked out on me, would she? Not after all this time!

Then the phone rang. It was a nurse at the hospital saying my wife had been taken seriously ill while shopping. She was in the emergency room and needed me to come as soon as possible. "No!" I remember thinking. "There must be a mistake. My wife was well when she left this morning."

I called a cab and paced the house while waiting for it to arrive. "Please, God, not Sylvia. I promise I'll never argue with her again, just don't let it be her." Minutes later I was at the hospital. The emergency receptionist pointed to a seat. I refused. "I've been asked to get here quickly to see my wife. I want to see her now. Will you please go and get the supervisor?" In my head I heard Sylvia's voice as she complained to her friend about me: "Gerald can be so embarrassing sometimes. He even demands to see the manager in restaurants."

The nurse who had phoned me appeared, and we went into a small room nearby. I asked how Sylvia was. "I'm sorry. She died ten minutes ago, just after I phoned. It was a massive heart attack." I was so angry. I shouted at her for not phoning me sooner. I criticized the hospital for incompetence, and then I demanded to see the doctor who had treated Sylvia.

"Why couldn't you save her?" Gently and calmly the physician explained that sometimes with heart attacks the damage is so great that there is nothing they can do. He told me they had tried everything in their power, but the damage was too great. I was trying to understand. But Sylvia had never had any heart problems. In fact, when they had treated her bowel cancer, everyone had said what good shape she was in.

The consultant was sympathetic. "People who have never had a day's illness can suddenly suffer a fatal heart attack. It's not common, but it happens."

It happens! It happens! The anger flared up again. This was my wife Sylvia he was talking about. The typical hospital cup of coffee arrived just then: "We're sorry Sylvia's dead; please have some coffee instead." The rhyme wouldn't go away. I started to laugh, somewhat hysterically, and then I began to sob. Not tears, but great, body-wrenching sobs.

I lost track of time after that. I called our two sons at some point and discovered one of them was on a business trip in New York and the other couldn't get here till late that night. I tried to call our pastor, but it was his day off. It was all turning into a nightmare.

They asked if I'd like to see Sylvia. "What on earth for?" I remember asking. The nurse persevered. "Of course you might not want to, but some people find it very helpful." I looked long and hard at her. "Young woman, what you've got to understand is that my wife and I argued this morning. I stormed off, calling her a forgetful old woman, and I never even said goodbye." I'll never forget what the nurse said then. "Well, perhaps now you can see her, tell her what you really think of her, and then you can say goodbye." I began to cry. I did see Sylvia. She looked really peaceful, younger almost. And I talked to her, told her that I was a foolish old man and that I hadn't meant what I said that morning.

I've never been the demonstrative type. When I was a boy, my father was killed in the Second World War, but I was told not to cry; he had died for his country and I should be proud of him. I was also told that I needed to be a man now and look after my mother. Chin up, son. I was only ten! Since then I've always kept a tight rein on my emotions. But sitting there beside Sylvia, my guard slipped. I felt such regret for the things I'd never told her—important things, like how much I loved her and really needed her. I just hoped that wherever she was she could hear me. Why did I have to wait until she died before I could tell her how much she meant to me?

It's now been eighteen months since Sylvia died. I realize how much I took her for granted. And when I look back, I just can't understand why she never left me. Then I think of how similar our backgrounds were. She would never have divorced me. It just wasn't done. So was she unhappy inside, or did she really like the crotchety way we rubbed each other?

After the shock with bowel cancer, I had realized how much I would miss her if she died. But you forget, don't you? As soon as she had recovered from surgery, I put it all behind me and things just returned to the way they had been before.

The days are so long now. I just can't fill them. I'm sixty-four years old. I retired at sixty and the future just stretches bleakly ahead. I see my sons about twice a year, play golf once a week, go to church on Sunday, and that's it. The sum total of my life. Great, isn't it?

Sudden deaths like Sylvia's often generate feelings of regret. Day by day we take each other so much for granted, expecting tomorrow to be the same as today. And then when it isn't, the things we'd like to have said, the things we'd like to have done, become "if only." Sure, it's all very easy to say, "Live each day as if it were your last!" But that's easier said than done. And if we went around expecting everyone we loved to drop dead from a heart attack any minute, the nervous strain would be enormous.

Gerald's sadness is that he still regrets so much. His childhood training that "big boys don't cry" has shaped the rest of his life. It is only now, when he has lost someone who had been at his side for all his adult life, that he realizes how much of himself he hid away.

We could have done so much more. Traveling, the theater, spending time with the children instead of sending them to boarding school. I look back now and ask myself what it was all for. We're born, we grow up, we marry, we have children, we work, we retire, and then we die.

Nearly my whole life I did what the "shoulds" told me: that good-old, stiff-upper-lip checking to make sure that I didn't enjoy myself too much, didn't feel too much. Sylvia's death taught me the futility of all that, and I so wish that she were here to share the discovery with me.

———◆◆◆———

Both of the accounts in this chapter reveal a lot of sadness and suffering. Both were heightened by the suddenness of the person's death. There was no time for preparation, or to tackle what is often called "the unfinished business." If Gerald had been able to have another twenty-four hours with Sylvia, he might have been able to express the things he'd always felt uncomfortable saying. If Joan had known that Chris would die—say in three months—she may still have a lot of grieving to go through, but those three months would have prepared her. Maybe her relationship with Chris's parents would have been maintained through her grief.

It just didn't happen that way. Neither Sylvia nor Chris could have realized what was happening to them, and the people closest to them were hit the hardest. When we are reeling from the intense bereavement of a sudden death, is there anything we can do to help ourselves?

The previous chapter described the processes and stages of grief. It is possible that some people will experience those stages much more intensely than others. Anger and disbelief are often more prevalent in situations of sudden death. Losing someone without warning or chance to say goodbye is deeply shocking. Enormous anger can get directed at people we feel could have prevented the death. Regret is one of the hardest things to handle in a sudden death. The things we wish we had been able to say, the future we wish we'd been able to share.... Some people find their level of regret is so great that it totally dominates their lives. In these circumstances a bereavement counselor may encourage writing a letter to the person who died, just as Joan wrote, expressing all the things the bereaved person wishes he or she had been able to say. Or the counselor might ask: "Imagine the person you're grieving for is sitting in that empty chair in front of you— what would you like to say to that person?"

These useful devices help articulate some of that regret which, at the moment, feels like a heavy load. Nobody promises that it will take away the pain, but it helps to identify just what are the areas of regret. Some of them might turn out to be completely unrealistic. It's no use wishing a relationship had been perfect. Relationships never are. We are, after all, fallible, sinful, and not always sensible human beings. Accepting this can help bring back a sense of proportion.

If there is a particular incident you regret or feel guilty about and find it won't leave your mind, try writing it out in a letter of apology. What do you do with the letter when it is written? Mail it to your therapist, counselor or spiritual director. Or take it to the graveside and read it aloud. Another possibility would be to burn it, thereby symbolizing that the incident is over. People who are part of a Christian tradition with sacramental reconciliation can find it helpful to confess formally and receive absolution from a priest.

We can also renew our belief that through Jesus Christ our sins are forgiven and read once more the account of Jesus and the woman accused of adultery (cf. Jn 8:1–8). In this story the scribes and the Pharisees brought her to Jesus, claiming that the law of Moses required that she be stoned as an adulteress. What did Jesus think? At first he appears to ignore the question. But when pressed, he states, "Let anyone among you who is without sin be the first to throw a stone at her." They all wander off, leaving the woman alone with Jesus. "Has nobody condemned you?" he asks. "No one!" "Neither do I condemn you. Go your way, and from now on do not sin again." Imagine that, instead of the woman in that story, you are the one who has been brought for condemnation for that incident you so regret. What is said about you? Who is condemning you? Maybe there is no one to condemn you but yourself. How do you feel?

Then move on in the story, to the point where all the accusers have to admit that, in some way, they too are guilty. No one else is without sin either. And then Jesus says to you, "Does no one condemn you? Then neither do I!" How does that feel? How do you want to respond?

If you followed the exercise but still feel driven by guilt, try to understand why you may be hanging on to that guilt. Unfortunately, people sometimes hang on to their guilt as a way of punishing or protecting themselves from feeling other equally strong emotions. Continuing to cling to guilt affects the way we feel about the future and prevents us from moving on and adjusting to life without the person who died.

For a Christian, to continue living with a feeling of condemnation is to deny the reality of the Gospel. No matter how terrible one may have been, God's forgiveness is there. To be really blunt, what makes us so "special" that we can somehow set ourselves apart from God's forgiveness?

These are tough words, but they are not meant to be unkind—quite the contrary. Real kindness to ourselves means facing guilt square on, looking it full in the face, and then having the courage to move on. If we have the strength to live daily with guilt, then we also have the strength to live without it.

It is also important to understand that we may need the help of a professional to find the root cause of persistent guilt. There is no shame or stigma attached to seeking such help, and many people have found that counseling has helped them to gain valuable insight into why they feel as they do.

One of the most tragic instances of sudden death is crib death, or Sudden Infant Death Syndrome (SIDS). New mothers acknowledge it as one of their biggest fears. Little is known about its cause and little can be done to prevent it. A baby can be put to bed one night looking perfectly healthy, and then found dead the next morning.

Nicola and Jack's story

The sad event of sudden infant death is exactly what happened to Nicola and her husband, Jack. Their son, Justin, was four months old on the day he was found dead. They had two older children—Timothy, aged five, and Sally, aged three.

Justin had always been a healthy baby, despite the fact that he was born three weeks prematurely. He had a huge appetite and sometimes I felt guilty that I didn't have enough milk for him. Jack would rub my shoulders when I said this, telling me that I was exaggerating, and that made a difference.

The day before Justin died had been so nice. We had gone for a family picnic on a warm, early spring day. Everyone was in a good mood and it was delightful to be together as a family. We brought the children home tired and happy, and all went off to bed without incident. Jack and I enjoyed the peace and quiet until about midnight, when Justin woke up crying. He wasn't quite as hungry as usual, but I didn't think anything of it.

It was just after 5:30 the next morning when I woke with a start, feeling very uneasy. The house seemed unnaturally quiet, and I felt compelled to check on the children. Timothy and Sally were sound asleep. But as I stood outside Justin's door, I felt this sinister intuition. Peering inside, I found Justin lying face down, so still. I knew he was dead.

I picked him up. There was no point in trying to resuscitate him. He had been dead some time. I sat on the floor in his room, rocking him gently from side to side. I stroked his hair. I wrapped him up to keep him warm. I sat there with Justin for what felt like the time-lessness of eternity. I didn't cry. I kept watch, in case, somehow, my son needed me.

Jack came. He took in the scene and knew immediately. He cried, and then I did too. Now I knew my link with Justin had gone. A doctor came, then the police. My baby was going to be taken from me. What were we to tell Timothy and Sally who were downstairs watching videos through all of this? They were more quiet than I can ever remember.

We told them together. We said that Justin had died, just like Grandma had last year, and that he had gone to heaven. Sally wanted to know why the doctor had come to look at him if he was in heaven. So we asked if they would like to see Justin and say goodbye to him, because he was soon to be taken to the hospital to find out why he had died. (As I said those words, I prayed they wouldn't ask how. They didn't; they were more interested in seeing Justin.)

When they came to take Justin for the autopsy, we were all in the living room. The children had each held him. Sally was quite matter-of-fact about the whole thing, wanting to know if he would be buried in the garden with Fergus, the cat, who'd died just last month. Timothy was more upset. When we first told him I was expecting a baby, he'd said he wanted a brother. And now he understood that his brother had gone.

One of the worst moments was when we had to register Justin's death, once his tiny body had undergone the autopsy. Just a short time ago we had been there proudly registering his birth. As I watched the pen recording the end of my dear son's life, I couldn't believe this was happening to us. It all seemed so unreal. Was Justin really dead? Was this all just a nightmare that I'd wake up from? But inside of me a deep, deep ache, coupled with a feeling like terror, told me it was all so horribly true.

The funeral was very simple. As Jack carried the tiny white coffin into the chapel, I couldn't help but remember the day that Jack had so cheerfully carried Justin from the car to our home, shortly after his birth. Now, less than four months later, our son was dead, and the autopsy had revealed no reason for it. Inside I felt so angry I thought I'd explode. How can a perfectly healthy baby just die?

People remarked how wonderful we were. Then we were expected to get back to normal. Normal? What's normal when one day your life revolves around a demanding infant, and the next there's nothing more you can do for him? He's gone.

My breasts ached and leaked with the milk I couldn't give my son. I looked in the mirror and saw someone who wasn't fit to be a mother. She had failed. She'd let her son die. When Jack tried to hold me, I shook him off. His touch was a reminder of the love which had conceived Justin and of which I was no longer worthy.

Three months later I still hated my body. I wouldn't let Jack near me. I was terrified something would happen to Timothy and Sally, and would never rest when they were out of my sight. One night Jack erupted. "You're not the only one who's lost a son, you know. I really feel for you, but he was my son too. It was a shock, but it was three months ago, and since then you've shut me out. I don't know what you're thinking. I don't know what's going on in your head. I can't bear the way you freeze when I touch you—like I'm a murderer. Tell me if you think I'm to blame for Justin's death!"

I remember staring at him. He thought he was to blame, but it was my fault, my body which hadn't been enough for Justin. I was the murderer. With that we started to talk, and we talked long into the night. We rediscovered our love for one another.

The next day we made an appointment to see our family doctor together. Helpfully she explained again what we already knew, but couldn't believe: that it wasn't our fault Justin had died. The room may have been too hot or too cold; it might have been better if he'd been put to bed lying on his back, but then the other two had survived sleeping on their sides, hadn't they? Finally I think we were both reassured. There was no real reason why Justin had died. It seems he took a breath and then, quite simply, forgot to take another. And no one can be blamed for that.

Guilt, anger, panic, anxiety, disbelief, confusion. They are all emotions that can turn us upside down and inside out. The world begins to feel like an unsafe place with all kinds of horrors just waiting to get us. The protective adult coat we wear, which is woven from confidence and experience, is ripped from us, and beneath that is the vulnerable child: unsure, ill-prepared, fearful. This is what bereavement can do to us, especially when death has been sudden and completely unexpected.

Then, one day we realize things have shifted almost imperceptibly. One day we may feel all right, the next may be bad, but the good times are getting longer. Through both the good and the bad we should treat ourselves gently. We must try not to deny the love which people around us are offering. If our grief is a grief they share, we must also try not to shut them out.

Sudden death rips our world apart. It is profoundly shocking. Disbelief, anger, numbness, and guilt become daily companions. And the question "why?" keeps recurring. Sometimes that "why?" can never be answered, and we can feel haunted by the fact that "we never even said goodbye!" At times there can be no words that will comfort, no thoughts that will ease the agony of endless questioning. Our only chance of survival and sanity may be to accept the love of others and allow ourselves to express the agony that is tearing us apart inside.

"You Can Always Have Another"
The Hidden Bereavements

I was thirty-two weeks pregnant when I began to worry that I couldn't feel the baby moving. The kicking had stopped. My obstetrician said not to worry; as babies grow, they get more quiet. I wasn't satisfied and phoned the hospital. They put me on a monitor, but then started to look worried. When the third doctor came in to try to find a heartbeat, I choked, "My baby's dead, isn't it?" He nodded. "I'm sorry, but it looks that way."

---◆---

Our baby lived just ten hours. He was born four weeks early. When I heard the urgent, whispered voices of the medical staff as soon as I'd delivered him, I started to worry. He was rushed off to the special-care baby unit, and they told us he was having difficulty breathing. Jack stayed with me for a while, and then went to find out what was happening. Just ten hours after he was born, our baby son died. They dressed him and wrapped him in a gown. Jack and I were able to hold him—for the first and last time.

Each year in the United States there are 26,800 stillborn babies and 900,000 early pregnancy losses. Sadly, these are often among the unacknowledged bereavements due to miscarriage (when a pregnancy is lost before twenty-four weeks), stillbirth, and neonatal death (death within twenty-eight days of birth). Suffering parents report that medical staff, friends, and relatives drop remarks like, "Never mind, you can always have another," or, "Well, it wasn't a real baby yet; don't upset yourself so much!"

Such clichés are probably said with the best of intentions. Nonetheless, they aggravate the feelings of people who are grieving the loss of their baby. From the beginning of the baby's development, parents nurture the new life. Then—it's gone.

Part of the problem seems to be language. Sometimes medical terminology—miscarriage, spontaneous abortion, the inviability of the fetus—disguises what the parents feel. To the father and mother, the simple fact is that their much-anticipated baby is dead. They may have seen their baby's moving image on a sonogram that intensified the awareness of the pregnancy: a baby is developing. They may have been reading the baby books that describe the different organs and the formation of fingers and toes. They could have begun to think about names. If it is a first child, they may have begun to daydream about having a child in the house.

And then, suddenly, it's all over. The woman is no longer pregnant. For some reason, and nobody may know why, she miscarried. With nothing to show for the pregnancy, the morning sickness seemed to be all in vain, and she feels tearful and sad. "It's because of sudden change in hormone levels," she might be told, but it is more than that. She is grieving her unborn child.

Suzanne and Graham's story

Suzanne worked as a teacher at the local elementary school. She had been there for ten years. Graham, her husband, was a sales representative for a large company and spent a lot of time away from home, traveling across the country. Two years before, they had decided it was time to start a family and had expected immediate success. A year later there was still no sign of a pregnancy, and they consulted their physician. She advised them to relax and, much to their embarrassment, checked that they knew the basic facts of life. She suggested they wait another year before seeking infertility investigations. Suzanne, at thirty-two, didn't want to wait. She wanted to know right away whether there was a problem, but the doctor insisted they wait another six months to let nature take its course.

Six months later there was still no pregnancy. This time the physician agreed to refer them, adding that the waiting list for first appointments was about a year. Suzanne exploded. Didn't the doctor realize how much they wanted a baby? The doctor shrugged it off unsympathetically.

Suzanne and Graham began some research and privately received an appointment at one of the top infertility clinics in the country. Suzanne realized how sensitive she had become. She became easily upset by television advertisements with mothers and bright, smiling children, or by the number of baby carriages along the road, or by casual questions from people at church—"No children yet?" Everything annoyed her. Suzanne was also conscious of how the calendar now ruled their lives. Graham planned his work around being able to get home for that critical time of Suzanne's cycle, and their lovemaking was turning into a chore.

Suzanne grimaced.

If I'd thought it was bad then, it was much worse once we had gone to the clinic. Temperature charts, sperm counts, and a whole barrage of tests awaited us. Some were quite painful, but in the end we knew that there was physically no apparent reason why I was unable to conceive.

During all this time, apart from me telling my best friend, we didn't breathe a word to anyone. At work I excused myself, claiming an upset stomach if I had to take a day off to keep an appointment. We had just met with a doctor who explained the various types of assisted conception available to us. We agreed to wait and talk things over together and with our pastor, when I realized I might be pregnant.

Maybe it was stress that was making me late, I thought. But after four days I couldn't wait any longer and went to the pharmacist to buy a home pregnancy test. I raced home from school knowing that Graham wouldn't be back for at least another two hours, and disappeared into the bathroom.

One hour later I knew. This was it. I was finally pregnant. Alleluia! I'd been beginning to think that God never intended us to be parents, but no, here was the proof. Graham was as crazy about the news as I was.

I kept on working, even with the morning sickness, and I tried to keep it quiet that I was pregnant. I looked so happy that people kept asking if I'd won the lottery or something. So, when I was eight weeks pregnant, I told them. Graham's and my parents were thrilled. It would be their first grandchild. A couple of people we knew from church told me they were glad we hadn't waited any longer. If only they knew!

My colleagues at work were pleased for us. I think my happiness showed how much we looked forward to this baby. I really knew the secret was out when one of my first graders piped up in class with, "Are you really going to have a baby?" "Yes," I said with a grin, forgiving her impertinence, "I'm going to have a baby."

Whenever I'd read the baby books I always skipped the chapter on miscarriage. It had taken so long to get to this stage, I couldn't believe God would let me lose my baby. My mind was completely closed to the possibility. So when, at sixteen weeks, I started bleeding slightly, I didn't say anything—not even to Graham. I couldn't bear to worry him. It couldn't be anything to be concerned about, surely?

Famous last words. Two days later, just after we finished dinner, I felt a sharp cramp, and then another, and within half an hour I was in a lot of pain. Graham called the doctor who admitted me right away to hospital. For the next two days, the bleeding got worse and then eased. The pain increased and then almost stopped. The ultra-sound showed that the baby's heart was still beating. I began to feel optimistic, but then at 3 a.m. I began to get terrible cramps and the bleeding began again.

I lay in bed pleading with God to stop what was happening. My tiny, tiny baby wasn't ready to be born. But as the pains kept coming, I felt despair. My prayers went unheard. Through the pain I could feel only desolation and terrible loneliness. No one could comfort me. The labor that should have brought the child of my dreams was killing my baby, expelling it violently to the outside world.

Afterward the doctor told me I'd been carrying a girl, but I didn't want to look. Now when I think about it, I'm still haunted by the fear that our baby girl had been somehow deformed. The doctor I asked later said that the baby had been normal, but a part of me still can't believe that.

I can't describe how I felt. When Graham arrived, after it was all over, I couldn't talk to him. I felt angry at him for not being there for me and, at the same time, I felt guilty that I'd "lost" the baby we both had wanted so much. Obviously he was upset, but he tried to hide it by being matter-of-fact and practical. That made me even more angry with him.

As I left the hospital one of the nurses approached me, touched my arm and whispered, "I know how you're feeling. I lost my first one too, but I have two healthy kids now." I just nodded, but inside I was resentful. She couldn't know how I was feeling. I didn't want any other baby. I wanted the one I had just lost.

Back at home I couldn't settle down. I kept asking God why, and then I began to feel more guilty. Maybe it was my fault. Maybe I should have stopped working and rested more, maybe it was something I'd eaten. Maybe, deep down, I didn't really want a baby. That was why I couldn't get pregnant, that's why I lost my baby. I know it's ridiculous, but all these thoughts kept coming.

One of the worst things was coping with other people. Our parents tried to be supportive, but I sensed how upset they were inside. I found myself feeling guilty that I'd failed to give them a grandchild. Then, at work, I felt like a failure. I felt the kids were thinking that I couldn't even have a baby, let alone teach them properly. I know it sounds silly, but that's how I felt!

I was weepy and tired. It was like I'd lost all my energy, and it was a real struggle to do anything. I got up in the morning, drove to school, did what I had to do, and then came home and went to bed. Graham started to become annoyed with me. He'd been really great to begin with, but he expected me to get over it by now and wanted to try to have another baby. It seems he had fallen for the popular myth that the best thing to do is to get pregnant as soon as possible—the "you can always have another one" school of thought. Had he forgotten how difficult it had been to have the first baby?

We had really wanted that baby. Every month that I found I wasn't pregnant had been such a disappointment. We had spent so much money, too, trying to determine why we couldn't conceive. We would have been good parents, I kept thinking, resentful of the newspaper accounts that told of babies being battered, abortion figures, and teenage pregnancy rates.

Two months after the miscarriage, Maureen, one of the women from church, whom I knew by sight but had never really spoken to, asked if she could come for coffee one evening. She said she'd had four miscarriages and wondered if I'd like to talk. I wasn't sure I could bear her story, but it seemed impolite to refuse. And deep down, I did want to know how Maureen felt.

I'll never forget the evening she came. It was so helpful. By sharing some of what she felt, Maureen encouraged me to talk, and I found I was able to tell her things
that I hadn't even shared with Graham. She talked of the
need to mourn, just as I would have if I'd lost anyone else
I loved. She described how, after she lost her fourth pregnancy, she had a short funeral service in the hospital
chapel. That amazed me. I never considered having a
funeral service for a miscarriage; but thinking about it, it
made sense. After all, it was the loss of a tiny human life.

Suzanne now looks back on that evening as a turning point. Recognizing her feelings of bereavement
helped enormously. She wasn't abnormal. If anyone
was abnormal, it was the people who tried to deny her
the feeling of such a loss.

Two years later Suzanne conceived again. Despite
the anxiety that she felt throughout the pregnancy, she
gave birth to a healthy baby boy.

Pregnancy is God's plan for the growth of new life.
The future of the human race depends on the desire to
have children, to create the next generation. Perhaps it
is the technological sophistication of developed cultures that considers miscarriage "a hidden bereavement." Family planning and life expectancy lead us to
believe that we can have children when we want and
that they will automatically live to a happy old age. In
poorer countries, life and death are much closer to
everyone's experience. People there are painfully con-

scious that they are not in control of their own destiny and are only too aware of the unpredictability of life.

Here in the Western world, we like to think that we are in control. Medical science has led us to expect so much. Suzanne, and many women in similar situations, have so much of their future pinned on their unborn children: hopes, dreams, the beginning of a new family. Yet with the death of their babies, they lose all of that future and, if not unrecognized, their loss is often dismissed or devalued. Failing to recognize miscarriage as a bereavement denies a woman the chance to mourn. As we saw in chapter three, unexpressed and unrecognized grief can be destructive to health and to relationships.

Only recently has the Church recognized that parents appreciate the opportunity to hold a simple religious service in memory of a prematurely lost new life. Simple services are available for parents who would like to use them. Some hospital chaplains also hold annual services for parents who have lost their babies through termination, spontaneous abortion, miscarriage, stillbirth, or neonatal death.

One of the most moving research interviews I can recall from my twenty years in broadcasting was with a woman in her fifties. At the age of twenty she had given birth to a stillborn baby in the twenty-seventh week of pregnancy. Her eyes filled with tears as she described how she felt about that event. Apparently she never saw the baby; it was taken away. When she asked if it was a boy or a girl, she was told not even to think about it: the baby was dead and it would be better if she forgot it. Since then, she said, she had been haunted by the memory.

The perceived wisdom of that time appears today as sheer callousness. Only recently have mothers and fathers been encouraged to hold their stillborn babies after delivery. Today some non-profit organizations, such as SHARE Pregnancy and Infant Loss Support, Inc., actively persuade health authorities and health professionals to recognize the need for parents to have the opportunity to grieve.

The following story demonstrates how attitudes have changed from those expressed in the previous account.

Gail and Harry's story

Gail and Harry brought in the New Year toasting the health of their unborn baby. It had been a normal first pregnancy, and in just ten weeks they would be parents. A few days after their celebration, Gail went in for a routine check-up, but was immediately admitted to the hospital. Two hours later she was told that her baby was dead.

Harry was with me by then, but neither of us could say anything. We were so completely shocked. The doctor said that the baby had died in my womb. They didn't know why. He was very gentle, compassionate and not at all embarrassed that both Harry and I were crying. He said he would leave us alone for a few minutes but then he'd be back to induce labor.

Labor! All my friends had told me the pain was bearable because you knew you were going to have a baby. But I had to go through it, knowing that I was going to deliver a dead child in the end. My body, the incubator of new life, was now a coffin.

Those twelve hours must have been the worst of my life, despite the painkillers I received. They may have eased the physical pain, but nothing could address my mental anguish. Time stood still, and we were frozen in despair for eternity. With no end to the torture, we were to endure it on our own. Harry felt that way too. We cried a lot, and he held me.

When our baby boy was eventually born, the midwife cried too. After a few minutes she handed him to me, but I couldn't look. Harry did, though, and cradling our son in his arms, he said, "Look at him, Gail, he's so small and perfect." "And dead!" I cried. I reached for the bundle and found myself looking at our son's tiny form. I touched his miniscule fingers, felt the softness of the palm of his hands. We were left in peace for a while—I have no idea how long—and together we cried for our dead son. We decided to call him William.

Harry comes from a church-going family. He wanted William to be baptized by the chaplain. It was a simple ceremony. I held William in my arms, and Harry held me. The chaplain's words washed over me, and afterward I felt calmer, as if we'd done something good for William.

I stayed in the hospital that night but left the next morning, never seeing William again. As we left I was given a leaflet on stillborn and prenatal death. The midwife who had delivered William gave me some photographs of him, a lock of his thin wispy hair, a copy of his hand and footprints, and an identity bracelet with the date and his weight: three pounds, two ounces. We were also given a certificate of stillbirth to be taken to the registrar's office within six weeks.

We really treasure those few things—they are all we have of our son. That's the tragedy of stillbirth. You carry a baby for weeks and months, you plan for its future, and then—nothing. No memories, no time together. Thinking back, it was so good to have the opportunity to see and hold William. He was so beautiful. He looked so peaceful, like he was sleeping. Of course, we had to leave the hospital without him. Driving away, with empty arms, was heartbreaking.

When I got home I went straight to the room we had been preparing for him and started touching everything: the cot, the blankets, the clothes. Harry and I did nothing but cling to one another and cried until we could cry no more. That night I picked up the first jacket I had bought in readiness for William and took it to bed with me, resting my cheek on it.

Before all this happened I had never had much time for religion, but now I found myself questioning the reality of God. Might it be true that our son William was in some kind of heaven, whatever that means? I was torn between wanting to make some sense of this, and opting for a fatalistic acceptance that it was "just one of those things." Even now I'm not sure what I really believe. Then, about a month after I was home from the hospital, still feeling incredibly upset and angry, I wanted to know what had happened to William's body. The hospital had said they would take care of everything for us. We had both agreed to leave it to them, but now I wanted to know.

Contacting the hospital chaplain seemed the best move. He was so good, inviting me over to talk. He also said that if I felt I couldn't go back to the hospital, he would meet me elsewhere. But I wanted to go back. I wanted to remind myself that I really had gone through the trauma; and walking back through the hospital doors seemed to be one way to do that. We met the next day, just the chaplain and me. (Harry was back at work and thought I was crazy to want to know where William was!)

The chaplain asked me how I was doing. At first I began with a noncommittal "Okay," but when he asked me why I wanted to know where William's body was, I really lost it. The anger, the resentment at friends who wouldn't talk with me, the guilt that I'd killed my own baby, and now my dread that he had ended up in a hospital incinerator...! On that count the chaplain was able to reassure me. All the stillborn babies were buried together at the nearby cemetery, and it was marked by a memorial stone that read: "Never forgotten. We miss you all."

He told me the story of the memorial stone. Three years before, only an unkempt corner of the cemetery marked the place with a few handmade wooden crosses. Then a group of parents decided that their babies should not be dismissed so lightly and approached the board of directors, who were very willing to set up the memorial stone. Since then the same parents gave the hospital a Book of Remembrance for parents to record their baby's name and to write an inscription.

I can't tell you the relief I felt! Here were people who were not prepared to have their babies ignored, people like me who'd wanted to know where their babies were.

◆◆◆◆◆

Gail and Harry visited the cemetery. They had William's name entered in the Book of Remembrance, and Gail started to attend the monthly support meeting for people who had been through a similar experience. She was gradually able to accept William's death. One year later she and Harry were expecting their second child.

This new baby will not be a replacement for William. He will always be our firstborn. When his new brother or sister is old enough to understand, we will talk about their older brother who died. What I still find very hurtful, though, is that people—friends and relatives—won't talk about what's happened to us. It's like they just don't care—which I'm sure isn't true. I seem to have lost a few friends through the experience. But from the monthly support meetings, I made some very good friendships. We have some sad experiences in common, and it's a tremendous support. Now I'm involved in research fund-raising with the hope that, in the future, what happened to me won't happen to anyone else.

The hidden bereavement of miscarriage, termination, stillbirth, or neonatal death is only gradually being recognized. Sadly, it has taken the voices of the bereaved parents to evoke from others a greater appreciation of their loss. There are still accounts of unfeeling behavior on the part of professionals: for example, a hospital chaplain who refused a distraught mother's request for a funeral service, claiming that there was no need for a baby born before twenty-eight weeks; or a doctor who lightly dismissed the death of an abnormal baby, leaving the parents feeling that they were wrong to mourn.

Grief is almost always a lonely and isolating experience, especially so for a miscarriage or stillbirth. Other than the medical staff, usually no one else has shared the experience of the loss. Grandparents and children lose the hope and expectation of a new family member; and I certainly do not want to detract from their disappointment and bewilderment, but it is the parents who uniquely experience the loss of the new life they were expecting. They are the ones with the tangible proof of their loss—their lifeless child.

The overwhelming sense of grief parents may feel is heightened even further when this is the first major bereavement that they have encountered.

Besides the inevitable overwhelming sadness, there will also be other deeply undermining feelings. The greatest of these is guilt—"I'm a parent. I should have protected my unborn child." Then there will be anger—"The doctors and midwives should have been more careful. They should have known something was wrong and prevented it." There will be a terrible sense of failure—"Healthy babies are born every day. I couldn't even manage that!" Lastly, there will be jealousy—"Why does she have a healthy baby and I don't?"

These are all powerful feelings that can last for a long time—certainly more than a matter of weeks or months—and, sadly, can be some of the most destructive. A significant number of couples whose first baby has died separate within the following twelve months.

Even for those who are well supported and whose relationship is not threatened, the grief remains to some degree.

Women whose babies died prematurely experience particular pain in the week of the original "due date." Originally anticipated as such a happy week, now it is simply endured. As other parents who shared prenatal classes or appointments show their healthy newborn baby to the world, indescribable pain arises from the question, "And what did you have?"

Anniversaries can also be particularly piercing. On the day when parents would have been singing "Happy Birthday" to their three- or four- or eight-year-olds, they recall instead the time that their baby died. Some parents will do something special to mark the day of would-be birthdays, Christmas, or anniversaries of the death, such as lighting a candle or walking together in a significant place—something that the parents and siblings find valuable as a way of saying "we have not forgotten our baby who died."

The key aspect of these types of "hidden" bereavement is the need to acknowledge that they have lost their baby. That is why funeral or memorial services, no matter how long after the death, can be helpful. A funeral service for a lost baby is sad and harrowing for the parents, yet it helps them deal with the reality of their loss. Seeing the little coffin may be the first time they truly realize that their baby did die. It was not a nightmare but is something dreadful that did occur and that they have to learn to live with.

Parents who never had a funeral service—years ago attitudes were not so enlightened—often suffer, being unable to focus their grief. They feel as if they are left in limbo, as if the event has not yet finished. Sometimes years afterward they wonder what happened to their baby; they feel they should have marked their child's existence. Such people can be said to be stuck in their grieving but can still do something about it.

Hospital records (particularly recent ones) may have photographs of the baby. Some hospitals do this regularly, should the parents ask for them later. But in whatever year the baby was lost, if the hospital agreed to take care of arrangements, it is usually possible to get in touch and ask what happened. A hospital will usually have an arrangement with a local cemetery, and inquiries can locate the baby's resting place: possibly a communal plot or memorial stone, which could be visited.

Sometimes five, ten, even twenty years after a stillbirth or late-term miscarriage, parents have found it useful to have a short remembrance service for the baby they lost. Throughout those years they may not have completed their grieving, and a service of remembrance is an opportunity for them to finally acknowledge the loss and experience some healing.

Lesley and Bob's story

Lesley had a stillbirth in 1979. She was ill after the birth and was given no opportunity to see her son. All arrangements were left to the hospital, and she returned home stunned to find that the whole episode was covered with silence. Friends, relatives, and neighbors avoided any talk of what had happened. Her grief was never allowed expression.

Twelve years later, suffering from depression, she realized she was still mourning for her son. She visited the hospital where he was born, and sympathetic staff showed her the records relating to her child's birth. She learned about the memorial services held in the chapel and decided to attend the next one with her husband, Bob.

As we arrived I was handed a card and invited to write in my son's name and the day he had died. This was then placed in a basket with cards from the other parents. The service began with the twenty-third psalm followed by a short reading and a few prayers—all very simple, but expressing the pain felt by parents with the commendation of their babies to God's love. Then the basket with all the cards inside it was placed on the altar, a symbol of our committing our children to God's care.

There were lots of tears. For Bob and me they were healing tears. We were finally acknowledging our grief for our son's death. It had been twelve long, unfulfilling years. At last, the emptiness left me.

For parents who believe that God is the source of all life and has a plan for their lives, a miscarriage or stillbirth can rock the foundations of that belief. Why would God allow them to conceive, plan for their child's future, and then have it taken away so suddenly and cruelly? This is especially so if the doctors or the autopsy results reveal no reason for the baby's death.

This was a key issue for Suzanne, whose story was recounted earlier in this chapter.

> I just couldn't accept that God had willed this to happen. God knew how much we wanted that baby and couldn't have taken it from us just to teach us a lesson! It seems almost blasphemous to say it was God's will. What sort of God would do that? If I had been ill, there might have been a reason. If the baby had been deformed, again God might have had a reason. But there was no reason. I was healthy, and the baby had been progressing normally.
>
> Then I started wondering more about my baby. Was she now in heaven? If my baby was with God, what was the point of never having lived on earth? I've always believed that life is a gift that allows us to grow and develop, emotionally and spiritually, but my baby had no chance of that.
>
> The questions swirled around my head. Why, why, why? Finally I had to confess I just did not know, and never would. But I'm confident that God shared in our distress and our anger; God didn't cause it. As a couple and as individuals we have grown through the loss of our baby. I do not believe the miscarriage happened just

to make us more mature and more loving to other people. That's just been the result.

The following words from the "Funeral Service for a Stillborn Child" are an appropriate way to end this chapter.

We gather here on what is for all of us a very sad occasion. We were looking forward to a time of joy and happiness, and now there are tears and grief. We are left with a feeling of emptiness. All that has happened seems futile and pointless. Our minds are filled with questions to which there appear to be no answers. And we are left feeling lost: so many things we do not know; so many things we do not understand.

But there are some truths we do know. We know that the God who made us, loves us; that he loves us always; that, through his Son, Jesus Christ, he has promised never to leave nor forsake us. And we know also that others before us have found that his strength is available for us, especially at those times when we feel we have no strength of our own.

7

"If Only It Had Been Me Instead!"
The Death of a Child

Our seven-year-old daughter was struck by a drunken driver. She spent four days in the hospital on life-support, then died. That was three years ago, and I still cannot accept it. She had so much to live for; her whole future was ahead of her.

I'm seventy-two years old and I never thought I'd have to cope with the death of one of my own children. Yet three months ago my youngest son died, aged forty. It's not right. He should have been burying me, not the other way around. I lost my husband just a year ago, but this is worse. My son had years of life ahead of him.

Our son was diagnosed with a brain tumor. A year later he died, aged ten. We're a Christian family, but I find it very hard to accept this as God's will. I read about other children being cured of their cancer, so why not my son? We learned so much from John and the way he coped with his illness, but his death was still senseless.

The death of a child of any age seems wrong. It is against the natural order. Children are meant to bury their parents, not the other way around. The death of a child represents the death of so much unfulfilled potential, so many hopes for the future. In Victorian times, families were large and child mortality was high. Today, with smaller families, a better standard of living, and longer life expectancy, the death of a child is a rare and deeply shocking event. Parents who have learned to live with the death of a child admit that you never recover from it—you just learn to live better with it.

Karen and Hugh's story

Patti was eight when she first became ill. Her parents, Karen and Hugh, thought at first that it was a passing virus. But a week later Patti was still listless and Karen began to worry. The family doctor said there was a lot of "it" going around and not to worry. When Patti still wasn't better a week later, Karen went back to the doctor. This time they took blood tests, and gave a quick referral to a university hospital in the city.

Even though I'd been concerned about our quick referral, I just couldn't believe it when the pediatric consultant identified it as leukemia. Patti couldn't be that ill. She didn't look it. Just that morning she'd been asking when she could go home. There had to be some mistake.

But there wasn't. I moved into special accommodations in the hospital to be close to Patti through the horrors of the next few weeks. When alone, I cried and cried, imagining what my daughter was going through. Endless blood tests, bone marrow tests, chemotherapy. Every time they prescribed more tests, I wanted to refuse. I hated the thought of what they were doing to her, and felt sick. They were doing this to my "baby"! But Patti was so brave, even when her hair fell out. All she said was that it made her one of the gang! (There were three children receiving chemo at the same time, and they were all quite matter-of-fact about it!)

The other children went into remission. Patti didn't. She died, quite suddenly, just two months after she was diagnosed. She had slipped into a coma the previous evening, and died at two o'clock in the afternoon.

How can I find the words to describe how I felt? Numb. Sick. Jealous of the parents whose children were now in remission. Angry. Looking back, it was like living on two levels. Outside I was the kind, loving mother successfully keeping her feelings under control; inside, I was being torn apart.

Before she died, Hugh and I sat with Patti all night and morning. We held her hand, talked to her, and practically willed her to wake up. I remember praying endlessly, bargaining with God: "Let Patti recover, and I'll try so hard to be good for the rest of my life!"

Then the doctor told us that there was no hope of Patti pulling through. His words hit me as if he'd thrown icy water all over me. I couldn't breathe, and I felt as if I were going to faint. Until then I had believed Patti was going to be all right, no matter what Hugh and the doctors told me. Now I had to admit that my daughter was dying.

I went in and sat on her bed, cradling her as much as I could. I could remember so vividly the day she was born—how frightened I was, but how excited at the same time. Then I had felt all joy and love as the nurse put Patti in my arms for the first time. It seemed like yesterday, but now Patti was leaving me, and there was nothing I could do to stop it. I couldn't cry, but my whole body was crying for me. My stomach cramped, my muscles ached, and I felt a pain in my chest that lasted for days.

Hugh and I talked to Patti. We told her she would be safe and that her Grandma and Grandpa would be waiting for her when she was ready to go. Her breathing dropped. As we told her how much we loved her, the inevitable moment arrived when we realized it was all over. Patti had died, quietly and peacefully.

I remember standing at the window, looking down on the world outside. It looked so normal. The sun was shining, there was a traffic jam, and people were walking decisively around with briefcases and shopping bags. Across the road a young couple stood holding hands and gazing into each other's eyes. Young love! That's when the tears began. Patti would never know what it's like to fall in love for the first time. She would never grow up; she would never be the airline pilot she always said she wanted to be. What a complete and utter waste.

The hospital staff were very kind and let us sit with Patti until we were ready to leave. A couple of the nurses who had been Patti's favorites and the young doctor who had spent a lot of time caring for her came in to say how sorry they were. My heart went out to them. There were so many really sick children in this hospital. Where did these professionals get the emotional strength to keep on caring?

Hugh suggested that it was time to leave Patti. I couldn't bear to go—thinking of her being wheeled off to a funeral home as soon as we left. But, after a while, we did leave. I left her favorite teddy bear lying next to her cheek and asked the nurse to make sure that Ted went with her. She agreed. I didn't want Patti to be completely on her own.

Then it was home to a quiet, empty house. Peter, our five-year-old, was staying with my sister, and now there was no Patti. Hugh and I just sat in the kitchen, staring into our coffee mugs, trying to postpone the moment when we had to tell everyone what had happened. We realized that once we had done that, it was for real.

I just cannot adequately describe those first few weeks. Although I had had time to think what might happen if Patti died, I had never really thought she would. I had met other parents whose children had been fighting leukemia on and off for years, and had built a lot of hope on that. I'd often talked with Hugh about going to Disneyland as a special treat when Patti was better.

Now I was torturing myself, wondering if I'd done something to Patti to cause her leukemia. Was it the food I'd given her? Or chemicals we'd used in the house? I would find myself sitting in her bedroom— which I just couldn't manage to change or do anything with—and would talk to her. I'd pick up her books, needing to touch something I knew she had touched. It made me feel close to her.

You'd have thought Hugh and I would have been able to support each other through the pain, but we barely talked. He went back to work soon and seemed to bury himself in his job. But I was at home all day, alone with my memories and thoughts. In the early days, right after Patti's death, some of our friends had been really good, visiting for hours, letting us talk and cry, and checking that we ate and had enough food in the house.

Except for Rose (an unmarried friend from school days), our friends gradually stopped coming over. They'd phone occasionally to "see if we were feeling better." Anyone would think we'd just had the flu—not lost a child! But Rose would come during her lunch breaks at least twice a week, and she'd let me talk about Patti. And when I cried, she didn't get embarrassed or immediately look at her watch saying she had to leave!

I'm not sure we handled our son Peter as well as we might have. When Patti was in the hospital, he had gone to see her. Then, when she'd taken a turn for the worse, he had stayed with my sister so that we could both be at the hospital. We only told him that Patti was not doing well and we wanted to be with her. He had asked if he could come too, but we had felt it was better that he stayed with his aunt.

After Patti died, we didn't know what to tell him. He seemed too young to be told his big sister had died, so we decided to explain that Patti had gone to live with Jesus and wouldn't be coming back. Peter didn't come to the funeral because I was afraid that it would upset him. To our alarm, when Hugh was leaving for a four-day business trip a few weeks later, Peter became very agitated and concerned that Daddy was "going off to live with Jesus" too. So then I had to explain that Patti had died. Later I took him to see her grave. We took flowers with us and he responded with enthusiasm.

But two days later, when I discovered him in Patti's bedroom going through her toys and games, I exploded. I didn't want anyone to touch her things. "But now

Patti's dead and with Jesus. She doesn't need them," he said. I broke down, screamed at him and sent him to bed while I sobbed in my own room. It hurts to tell that story, because I reacted like a monster. I suppose I was one, and I feel so guilty about it.

I was so wrapped up in my own grief that I couldn't cope with others' feelings. Even though I neglected Peter emotionally, I thank God that he is normal today! As for Hugh, I completely excluded him. He used to get impatient with me when he came home from work and found me in tears. In turn, I would lash out at him. How could he be so matter-of-fact about his daughter's death?

◆◆◆

Karen and Hugh's marriage had virtually disintegrated by this time. Six months had passed since Patti's death, and the grief was still very raw. Karen's friend, Rose, was concerned and investigated some kind of assistance for them. She phoned the local social services and discovered a bereavement counselor. The next step was to persuade Karen and Hugh to agree to see her. Much to Rose's surprise, Hugh jumped at the opportunity; but Karen still needed encouragement. Let Hugh now explain why.

I knew we were in trouble. I couldn't get close to Karen. She was always crying and wouldn't let me touch her. I was feeling guilty that I had failed as a father by letting Patti die. I was supposed to have protected her, and now I couldn't even comfort Karen. It was obvious we had to talk with an impartial professional.

I was angry with Karen. She was moping around as if she were the only one who was grieving, but I was too. Men are brought up to hide their feelings, not to cry—they're taught to be strong. At work I could keep my head down and ignore my pain. Besides, somebody had to bring the money in, otherwise we'd have been homeless as well.

One of the good memories I have from when Patti was in the hospital was a week or so before she died. Karen was at her sister's with Peter, so it was just Patti and me on our own. She was very weak by this stage and couldn't really walk. She just looked straight at me and said: "Daddy, I'm going to die, aren't I?"

How on earth do you tell your daughter that, yes, she's dying? But I couldn't lie to her either. She was bright, she knew what had happened to one of the other children with leukemia. So I took a deep breath and told her the truth as gently as I could. I held her hand as we talked, but then realized it was Patti who held my hand. My dying daughter was trying to comfort her father! She sighed and said, "I hate being sick, Daddy. I don't even want to play anymore. But when I go to heaven I'll be better."

She paused and then went on, "Mommy keeps telling me I'll get better. Don't tell her I know I'm going to die. She'll be so upset." We hugged each other then, and I read to her before she fell asleep. Afterward I didn't know what to do. Patti had been right. Karen refused to believe that Patti was going to die. The doctors had talked to us several times already, obviously trying to prepare us for our daughter's death, but it was as if Karen couldn't hear what they said. I knew that when the inevitable happened,

Karen was going to take it very hard. But I didn't know how to prepare her.

That night I tried to talk to her about the prospect of Patti dying, but Karen screamed at me, saying I'd given up hope. We had to will her to live! So I gave up. I had two more chats with Patti, on my own, before she slipped into a coma. I'll cherish those chats forever. She knew what was happening and wasn't at all afraid. "I'll just go to sleep and not wake up." And the very last time, as I left she said, "Tell Peter I'm sorry that I was so mean to him. Bye-bye, Daddy. I love you." I'm sure she knew that was the last time she'd see me.

My faith isn't very strong, but Patti taught me not to fear death. And what's more, I now believe there is life after death and that Patti will be there waiting for me when I die. I've started going to church sometimes, but Karen won't come with me. I tried to tell her about the conversations I'd had with Patti, but I think she feels guilty that she couldn't talk to Patti about it all.

Our marriage became a disaster. Karen and I couldn't communicate. People said, "At least you have each other." That was a joke. We may have been living in the same house, but we didn't "have" each other. I wished we did. We needed each other. As for Peter, he not only lost his sister, even his parents were falling apart!

Karen and Hugh did go to see a bereavement counselor—together at first and then separately. They also went to a support group. They met other parents who knew what it was like to lose a child, and drew enormous support from that shared grief. Some months later, Karen was able to see a difference in the way she felt.

I still miss Patti enormously, and it doesn't take much for me to cry, but I think our marriage has recovered. In counseling one day I had an image of Patti in my head: she was crying because her mommy and daddy were arguing. That had happened when she was about six, but suddenly I was thinking about what she would make of us now. She would have been so upset.

I feel much closer to Hugh now. He's talked to me about Patti in her last few days and what she said. He's right: I do feel guilty that I wasn't able to talk with her about her death. But I'm glad he managed to talk to Patti, or rather, that she was able to talk to him. It has also helped me to talk with other parents. Sometimes I still have bizarre thoughts. Sometimes I think I'm going crazy, but when you hear somebody else say the same thing after losing a child, you realize it's normal to feel as you do.

The group has also helped me think about how difficult it is for fathers when a child dies. All their upbringing is about being strong and protecting their family. Their grief is just as real, but they're brought up not to show it. I think that's worse. My advice for any other couple going through the grief of losing a child is this: whatever else you do, don't exclude one another. Let each other grieve in the way you need to, but share what you can. That's the time you need one another.

◆◆◆

Hugh and Karen are surviving together, but their story shows how easily couples can be torn apart by the death of their child. The strongest of relationships can be tested by overwhelming grief. When you most need each other, you become so absorbed in your own grieving that communication breaks down. Then alienation and isolation quickly take root. Friends and colleagues find it difficult to know what to say. Bereavement brings powerful feelings that cut you off from other people. Wrapped in grief, the world outside seems far away—distant and removed. It's hard to hear what is said, and even more difficult to connect with it.

In the middle of such unaccustomed behavior and reactions, it is worth struggling to hold on to one another. One woman described her relationship with her husband, after the death of a teenage son, as being "shipwrecked." Thrown into the raging sea on two flimsy bits of wood for security, they could just about link hands and support one another. But as the waves then broke around them, the fragile grip they had on one another slipped. "Before we knew it, the currents of bereavement had parted us, and we couldn't even see or call to one another!"

Even Christian parents have problems and burdens: feeling guilty that their faith is too weak, or angry that God has "taken" their son or daughter. They may feel enraged and abandoned by God.

Ultimately it is best to be honest about what we think and feel. Rather than censor our words and feelings to meet our theological expectations, it is far better to accept our inability to make sense of our child's death. We can then share our confusion with God in prayer. Even if our rage and anger make it impossible to pray with words, God will certainly be with us. In our deepest groans and cries, no matter how inarticulate and despairing we are, we will find the Holy Spirit's action at work. At the very bottom of the blackest pit, there is a rock on which to stand.

To our human thinking, the death of any child is a senseless waste. There has been no time to develop into adulthood, no opportunity to enjoy all that the world has to offer. Learning to read, to question, to think independently—there's so much out there to discover. Is there any purpose to lives that are cut short?

The answer has to be a resounding "yes!" At one funeral service, the presider offered the following reflection to the mourners of an eighteen-month-old baby girl. This child, he said, had lived a complete life. It had a beginning and a middle and an end. Although it was only eighteen months, it was a full lifespan, entire in itself. Grieving this loss deeply was right and necessary. But to consider the child's life "cut short" would deny its fullness and would minimize all the love and growth that had surrounded that child.

What is the special gift of these children to us? Are they purer souls than we are—already spiritually mature enough to move on? Some parents would categorically say yes—especially for children whose death was preceded by illness. These parents feel that they have seen their child grow spiritually. In younger children this is seen more in the way they handle their illness than in any perception of what life might mean. And older children, who understand the concept of their own death, can show a wisdom and an acceptance that seems to extend far beyond their years.

Jeff and Rachel's story

Jeff and Rachel are strong and active members of their local church. They had been unable to have a child of their own because Rachel had undergone a hysterectomy for endometriosis when she was twenty-eight. They had always wanted children and adopted Greg when he was just a few weeks old. In no time at all, Jeff and Rachel thought of Greg as their own son. They made no secret of the adoption, and Greg knew he was their special and much-wanted son.

Greg was a sunny and happy child. He always wanted to know the why of things. Why did birds fly, but people didn't? Why wasn't it summer all the time? Greg also liked to help people. After he joined the Cub Scouts, the family joked about the time he had picked all the daffodils in the garden and sold them to his friends for Mother's Day. Then he had given the proceeds to the local charity that the Cubs were supporting. Rachel had not been amused—at least not until the next day!

Time after time Jeff and Rachel thanked God for the gift of Greg. They marveled at how full of life he was and how much joy he brought them. Years before, when they had so desperately wanted a child, they had never imagined how good it could be to have one.

Greg talked quite naturally about God. He sang in the church choir and happily took part in daily family prayers. When he left for Scouts, on the evening after his eleventh birthday, he was his usual happy self. But thirty minutes later he was back. He said that he had fallen off his bike, braking suddenly to avoid a cat, and that he had hit his head. He was white and shaken.

Rachel decided to take him to the emergency room immediately. She was worried; and she became even more alarmed when Greg said that he thought he was going to die, but that she and Jeff shouldn't be too upset. "Of course you're not!" was Rachel's response, but inside she was praying, "Lord, don't let this be serious."

The doctor was reassuring, but said they would keep Greg overnight for observation—he had obviously suffered a nasty knock to his head. Rachel and Jeff sat with him for an hour, but then Greg said he was fine and that they should go home and get some rest. As they left he kissed them both and thanked them for being the best parents in the world.

Rachel was completely unnerved and couldn't settle down when she got home. She started to read her Bible, quickly coming across Isaiah 43: "Do not fear, for I have redeemed you; I have called you by name, you are mine. When you pass through the waters, I will be with you; and through the rivers, they shall not overwhelm you; when you walk through fire you shall not be burned, and the flame shall not consume you. For I am the LORD, your God."

About midnight Jeff went to bed, but Rachel stayed up. It was a beautiful night outside, warm and tranquil, and she took a light blanket to the garden and sat there, sometimes praying for Greg's safety, sometimes just keeping a watchful vigil.

At 2:15 a.m. the phone rang. It was the nurse, asking them to return to the hospital. Greg had taken a turn for the worse and they might have to operate. At the hospital they learned that Greg was now unconscious; the medical team feared that his skull was bleeding internally, requiring immediate surgery to relieve the pressure on his brain. Rachel and Jeff were allowed just a few minutes with him, before he was wheeled off to the operating room. Rachel sensed that she would never see Greg alive again.

I felt so helpless. It was dreadful watching them wheel him away. But as he went I sensed peace flow through my body. I can't really describe it, but when the peace came I was able to pray silently: "Lord, not my will, but yours be done."

◆◆◆

Rachel's intuition was correct: Greg died on the operating table. When the doctor came to the waiting room just after 4:30 a.m., Rachel was able to say, "Greg died a short time ago, didn't he? It's all over."

Looking back over the year since Greg died, Rachel and Jeff firmly believe that they have grown closer together. Here is an excerpt of the letter they sent out with their Christmas cards, just six months after Greg's death.

Thank you for all the wonderful letters and cards you sent us after Greg's death. It was so comforting to know that you were praying for us in our sad loss, and we want to tell you how much we have felt upheld by God's love throughout our grief. Our mourning has not quite been turned into dancing yet, but we are at least able to hear the music, and our feet are beginning to tap again!

We have spent the last six months trying to make sense of why Greg died. He had a bright future ahead of him and we loved him dearly. It was such an accidental death, and we keep asking ourselves if the hospital neglected to diagnose Greg's internal bleeding before it was too late. But none of that will bring Greg back. We have prayed and talked long and hard about the meaning of Greg's death, and know only that we believe it was somehow part of God's plan.

During his short life, Greg gave us so much love. Despite the pain of the last six months, we don't for one moment regret adopting him over eleven years ago. Greg was the child we could never have. It's as if God loaned him to us, to be loved and cared for as we grew as parents.

This Christmas will be a sad one, our first without Greg. But as we quietly celebrate the gift of the Christ child to the world, pray for us, that we can continue to thank God for the gift of Greg to us for those eleven short but wonderful years.

Rachel and Jeff's faith is remarkable. Their ability to thank God for Greg's short life, while readily admitting their lack of understanding, is a tribute to their faith. Their grief has been no less then anyone else's, and they are quick to admit some very dark days. Faith should not be the spiritual tranquilizer of believers—they too must mourn. Instead, faith enables us to believe in the timescale of God's purpose, even if we cannot see it.

I do not believe that God causes children to contract life-threatening and fatal illnesses, or to have accidents. The world was created by God, and human beings fall prey to viruses and germs. Scientific research is beginning to show that environmental damage caused by the human race contributes to an increase in certain types of cancer, for example. So, whose "fault" is it? God's or ours?

Arguments about accidental deaths are equally spurious. We are not puppets with the strings of our lives pulled by a divine puppeteer, but human beings living on this planet within the laws of nature. If a three-year-old who pulls free of her father and races into a road is fatally injured by a car that happens to be passing by, no one can say that God willed that child to run into the road. It was the personality and natural inquisitiveness of the three-year-old, coupled with her inability to know the risk, that attracted her into the road. If there had been no car or her father had joined her to look at the object in question or had scolded the child, it would have been a different story. If the car had arrived moments earlier or later, again the child might have survived. But at that particular millisecond, in that particular sequence of events and people, the child was hit.

Of course, if it is impossible to accept that God willed it to happen, or didn't prevent it from happening, then the difficulty comes in living with the randomness of that particular set of circumstances. Are we really as prey to the effects of random action as we are to germs and viruses? Are we, in effect, on our own in this accident-laden world?

To say we are on our own is too stark and simple. We have free will; we have the freedom to make our own choices. When we, or someone we love, is in the wrong place at the wrong time, we have to accept the consequences of this. It's not that God doesn't care or doesn't have a plan for us. We are simply subject to the natural laws of this world. That is a part of the mystery of life.

Within this mystery, and freedom of choice, the very essence of our humanity is found. Life is fragile and precious. We are not slaves to a tyrannical God who dictates our every move, but the children of a God who was born into this world as a vulnerable infant. Never distant or remote, God is present in our fragility and pain. God hears and shares in our raw vulnerability.

Is any of this comforting to a parent who is grieving for a child?

Never a simple puzzle, life is full of unanswered questions, and that is where faith can be important. Making any real sense of a child's death may seem impossible. What we can believe is that the God of limitless love is right beside us, through all the pain and relentless slaughter of our emotions. Just as Mary wept at the foot of the cross, seeing her Son's agonizing and humiliating death, we too will weep. But as the months turn to years, some sense of perspective will return and, in time, either in this world or the next, we will understand more fully the purposes of God.

8

Taboo Deaths
Difficult Circumstances

Alcohol ruled my mother's life and killed her. Sometimes she managed to stop drinking. The doctors said if she drank again, it would be the end—her liver would give up. She was doing fine, but then she was laid off and hit the booze. Six weeks later she was dead. People are sympathetic when you say your mother has died. But when you say she drank herself to death, their faces drop.

My brother was homosexual. My parents threw him out when he told them. I stayed in touch with him, though, and four years later I went to see him. He looked thin and pale. That's when he told me, "I've got AIDS, Jenny." I left home so I could be near him. Seven months later he died. I was with him and so was his partner, Jack.

My husband took his own life. I didn't even have a clue that anything was wrong! The police told me they found his car with the engine running and the hose from my vacuum cleaner attached to the exhaust, running back into the car. He left a note.

It didn't say much, just, "Sorry. I just couldn't take it any more."
Now, when people ask me how my husband died, I just say it was
a car accident.

Death is already a fairly unmentionable topic of conversation. The kinds of deaths described above, however, are even more taboo. People may offer sympathy to the newly bereaved, but there's definite censorship at any suggestion that the person may have been responsible for his or her own death. This censorship doesn't make sense, of course: if a man dies because he was driving too fast, the recriminations are few, if any. It's treated more like a case of bad luck! But if the same man deliberately drives his car into a brick wall at fifty miles an hour, his friends and acquaintances may look upon him in a distinctly unfavorable light. His immediate family can feel stigmatized and outcast. Both deaths are within the realm of personal responsibility, but it is the lack of a will to live that society cannot accept.

Duplicity about taboo deaths is all too evident today. Lung cancer as a direct result of smoking is all right; death from heroin addiction isn't. A heart attack is acceptable despite a lifetime habit of eating fats and an extra forty pounds of weight; drinking oneself into liver failure is not. Why do we discriminate? A death, however it is caused, is a death. The people who were close to the deceased, regardless of the cause of death, will grieve. Yet their grieving is heightened by being forced into even greater social isolation.

Angela's story

Angela and Tony were stalwart members of their local church. They lived in a beautiful little village in a picturesque part of the country. They had just one son, Roger. At eighteen he began studying medicine at a university. Angela was glad he had decided to become a doctor, since he was always very caring, even in early childhood. From time to time Tony had nagged Roger, claiming he was too soft for his own good and needed to toughen up. When the other boys in the neighborhood were out playing football, Roger preferred to read. But in his mother's eyes, it paid off. With straight As and highest honors, he had his choice of the finest medical schools.

I missed Roger enormously when he went off to school, but he phoned every week and came home when he could. He seemed to enjoy university life. He got involved in the campus ministry and had no problems with his exams at all. Passed every time.

I always encouraged him to bring his friends home. We have a large house with lots of space, and I would love to meet his friends. But he never brought them. Tony used to quiz him about girlfriends, but he just said he was too busy. He was looking tired and strained, but he said he was all right. That summer, before his second year, he announced he was going to work in Montreal. He wanted to improve his French.

I was disappointed. I had so looked forward to having him at home for three months, but I put on a brave face. He had his own life to live! But when he came back from Montreal, Roger looked different. He was more

confident, and the slight stammer he'd had since childhood was gone.

That Christmas he asked if a friend named Martin
could come to stay. Martin was a law student and his
parents lived in Georgia. It was too expensive for him to
go back for Christmas. I was delighted: not just one, but
two boys to mother over Christmas. Martin was a wonderful young man: very good-looking, very polite, and
he often used to wander over to the church to play the
organ. He was much better than our regular organist.

We had a lovely Christmas but then, on New Year's
Day, we were invited to friends. Martin and Roger came
too. Nothing improper happened there, but on the way
back, Tony was really subdued. He said that he wanted
to talk to Roger privately. Martin and I sat down in the
kitchen with a mug of coffee. Soon I became aware of
raised voices. Then Tony stormed in, ignored Martin,
and announced he was going out; when he returned, he
hoped that Roger would be gone! Then Roger came
into the room. Very calmly and lovingly he told me that
he was gay and that he was in love with Martin. They
both knew the church condemned homosexuality, but
they couldn't deny how they felt.

I felt devastated—not so much by what Roger had
told me, but by the way his "coming out" destroyed our
family life. Tony insisted that he never wanted to see or
talk to Roger again. I never hid the fact that I remained
in touch with Roger. I managed to see him for an occa-
sional weekend, but he never came home for Christmas
or birthdays like he used to. It broke my heart that
there was such a split.

We never told our friends what had happened—just
said that we'd drifted apart. I think something inside of

me died. I couldn't reject my son. This wasn't what I would have chosen for him, but he was a good young man. I couldn't label him a pervert like Tony did. Roger continued to do well at school; he and Martin started to live together.

Some years later Roger phoned me one day and asked if I could visit; it was urgent. He sounded tense and distant, and I was worried.

It was then that the whole sad story emerged. A few months earlier, Martin had discovered he was HIV positive, and now Roger was, too. Just that day, after much thought, he had given up his career in medicine. The risk to his patients was minimal, but he felt he couldn't hide his situation.

My heart broke for him. His sexuality had cost him his family, and now it had cost him his career. I feared that it would soon cost him his life.

Four years later Martin died from AIDS, and Roger began to show symptoms of the disease. He grieved deeply for Martin, and I felt powerless to help Roger as he struggled with the loss of the man he loved. He received a lot of support from other gay friends, but he was bitter that Martin's parents, who had come up from Georgia, had forbidden him to attend Martin's funeral. I couldn't believe that anyone could be that cruel, but Roger said such things were commonplace in the gay community. Several of his friends had undergone similar kinds of rejection.

Then, as Roger became sicker, he told me he was desperate to make his peace with his father. And, after all those years of turning his back on his son, Tony relented. Roger came home. I was delighted, but it was obvious that he was now very ill. He was extremely thin, very uncertain on his feet, and the childhood speech impairment had returned. I could tell Tony was extremely shocked by his son's condition. All of a sudden he began to cry, grabbed hold of Roger, and just held him close. "Stay with us, son. We'll look after you—get you fit and strong again!"

Roger looked straight at him and very softly said, "Dad, I'll never be fit and well again. It's gone too far. It's just a matter of time. It might be weeks, it could be months. But that's all." I've never seen Tony so out of control! He was in tears, berating himself for disowning his son, and asking forgiveness. That's when father and son embraced, for the first time in seven long years.

Tony and I had to think about what to say to other people. We could say that Roger had cancer. (Well, in one sense, he did.) But to do that was to deny what Roger and all of us were living with. I felt there had been too much denial already and wanted people to know the truth. So we did tell the truth, but it was terrible.

We discovered that many people are very judgmental about AIDS. Maybe it's because they are irrationally afraid that it is contagious; or because they condemn homosexuality. Whatever the reason, we realized we were on our own. Tony found that people who had been golfing partners for many years were suddenly unavailable for a game. I walked into the local grocery store, and the whole place fell silent. No one would meet my eye. My cleaning lady phoned to say that she was very sorry but she couldn't come any more: she "didn't want to pass it on" to any of her own family. Invitations to go out for dinner dried up, virtually overnight, apart from one person—Deidre, a dear lady in the next town who had been widowed a couple of years earlier. Locally she'd always been regarded as pretty eccentric, but I began to realize that for her, "eccentric" meant "accepting."

Deidre asked all three of us over for Sunday lunch. We hadn't been to church. I felt too angry to worship God with all those people around who didn't want to know us anymore. Instead, at Roger's suggestion, we had had a short time of prayer together. Over lunch at Deidre's that day, I realized that it felt good to be together as a family. And Deidre? Her toast was "to social pariahs, everywhere."

I could not have made it through the next several weeks without her. She knew about social isolation, she said, because since she had been widowed she'd realized that life revolved around couples. Deidre knew about loneliness and having to find the strength to carry on. She would come over and spend time with Roger, often reading to him, because his eyesight was beginning to go. She'd help with the cleaning or the shopping, but above all she was just there—ready to listen, non-judgmental.

The only other people who stayed in touch were two of Roger's friends—Sam and Timothy. They phoned almost daily, and stayed over one weekend. I thought I'd feel uncomfortable with them, but it turned out to be a very special time. Sam told me how painful it was to attend the funeral of a partner and be forced to remain at the back of the chapel, hoping that the family hadn't noticed. When I first heard stories like that, I was incredulous. Now, with our own experience, I have learned that Sam's account is not unique.

Another support for all of us at this time was our family doctor. He called in nearly every day, answered our questions as best he could and, if he didn't know the answers, would look them up. As Roger began to fail, it was he who found a hospice fifty miles away that could take Roger. I wanted to keep our son at home and let him die with us, but Roger himself insisted that he should go to the hospice. He said the end would be awful. He didn't want us having to nurse him through that.

So, about four months after Roger came to live with us, he left again—this time for good. We all knew it, but we were also able to talk about it. The strength of our small family at that time was inspiring. Thrown together, we had grown together.

Roger lived just twenty-four days after that, and by the end I was praying that God would take him. Tony and I had moved into a hotel near the hospice so that we could spend as much time as possible with Roger. He deteriorated rapidly. His eyesight had gone completely and he began to suffer terrible convulsions.

Roger had been right. The end was awful. Self-righteous people who claim that AIDS is God's judgment on sinful people, and who treat the whole family like lepers, should spend time at the bedside of an AIDS patient. Is God so vengeful and morally indignant to send such a horrific disease as a punishment?

No! The God I saw at work in that hospice was in the staff who so lovingly nursed my son, with no revulsion or prejudice; in the chaplain who spent so much time with Tony and me, encouraging us to talk about what we felt; and, of course, in dear, lovable, eccentric Deidre, who was there for all of us, all the way through.

Roger's funeral was small, shared with the hospice staff. The service, led by the chaplain, was honest. It expressed the tragedy of a young man's life, with so much potential, so horribly extinguished; but of our relief, also, that his suffering was now over.

And the future? Tony and I returned to our family home, but together decided we could no longer bear living there. The house felt welcoming, but not the neighborhood. The community had ostracized us at the very time we most needed support. I kept thinking how different things would have been if we had just said that Roger had cancer. And that sickened me. When someone is dying, they need support and love, as do their family.

I look back at the time Tony and I struggled to come to terms with Roger's illness and death, and still feel very angry at our so-called friends and acquaintances who rejected us. We were cast out as "untouchables," and that hurt—deeply.

◆ ◆ ◆

Angela's story is similar to so many others—not only those who suffer from AIDS, but also suicidal death and death from drug or alcohol addiction. These can all lead to the overwhelming isolation of those left grieving, even though they may have their own conflicting feelings of anger, guilt, or revulsion. A judgmental society withdraws support when it is most needed.

Fear or a sense of moral rectitude can make society behave so harshly. Yet, in the New Testament, again and again we read that Jesus spent time with the people who were considered unclean. He knew the foibles and fallibility of human beings, but he didn't avoid them. He talked instead about fullness of living and a better way of loving.

Steven's story

For Steven, it was not so much the disapproval of other people that was hard to take, but his own tremendous feelings of guilt. He was thirty-four when his wife, Penny, committed suicide. They had two daughters aged eleven and nine at the time.

Penny hadn't been herself for a couple of months. She wasn't sleeping well. I would find her sitting downstairs, gazing into the distance. It was like she was in another world. She wasn't listening when the girls told her things that had happened at school, and she stopped taking an interest in her appearance. Her hair needed washing, and she stopped wearing make-up.

I got really fed up with her behavior. It seemed selfish, and I couldn't see why she wouldn't make an effort. At times I tried to talk with Penny about what was going on, but she never said much and I ended up getting even angrier. I couldn't understand what was happening and felt very confused. If I tried to touch Penny, just to cuddle with her, she recoiled.

I encouraged Penny to go to a doctor. When she did eventually go, all he said was that she should pull herself together. Maybe she could get a job, so she'd have less time to think about herself.

When I heard this, I felt relieved that there was nothing wrong. But I got even more irritated by Penny and the way she was making life so miserable for the rest of her family. She and I got to the stage where we didn't really talk anymore, and I noticed that the girls started to avoid her. Right after their snack, they would go out with their friends or up to their bedrooms. "Mommy's no fun anymore!" one of them said.

I was at my wits end. I had no idea what was the best thing to do. I even thought about walking out, leaving her to get on with her life. Maybe that would shake her into action. But I couldn't do that to the girls.

Penny's parents had both died when she was sixteen, but she had a sister who agreed to come over. But she was exasperated that she couldn't get through either. When I look back, I can see why we got so angry and irritated. The physician had said there was nothing wrong, and so we expected Penny to "pull herself together."

After a while Penny appeared to get better. She dressed nicely, and even had lunch with a friend or two. She made more effort with the meals at home, and began smiling again. I was relieved that, whatever the problem had been, she now seemed to be getting over it. She still wasn't sleeping very well, but it didn't seem to worry her so much.

Then one day at work I got a call from Leila, our older daughter. Did I know where her mother was? She wasn't at home when they returned from school, although she had said she would be. I began to feel uneasy. Maybe Penny had just given up on us and walked out. I left for home right away. There was no note left behind, and none of her belongings were missing except her handbag. I couldn't understand where she was. I phoned everyone I could think of, but no one had seen her. I talked to the neighbors, and one of them said she had seen Penny walking down the street just after two o'clock.

By nine I was frantic. Then the police arrived. They gently explained that a woman had been killed by a train early that evening. My wife's handbag had been found at the scene. They asked if my wife had been depressed recently.

I couldn't quite make sense of their words. Why was Penny on a train? Why were they asking if she'd been depressed? How had she come to lose her handbag? Gently the officer explained that the woman they thought was Penny had deliberately walked onto the track as the train was coming. No! Not possible! Penny would never do that—it couldn't be her. There had to be some mistake!

It was Penny. I had to identify her by her clothes and jewelry, because her body was so badly mutilated by the train. When I heard myself saying that those were Penny's things I was hit by an enormous wave of guilt. Why hadn't she said she felt so awful? Why couldn't she have told me she was thinking about suicide? If I'd known I would have been more sympathetic. I hated myself because I had been so angry with her.

And then I thought of the doctor who had told her to go and find herself a job. If he had been standing in front of me then, I swear I would have punched him. Why hadn't he taken her seriously? Then I thought that I could have gone with her that time. Maybe he would have listened to me. And why hadn't I gone? Because I'd been busy at work. If only, if only...

There were so many ordeals to face after Penny's suicide—trying to explain it to the girls and then coping with the guilt and anger they felt; the investigation, the train driver who had come out of a tunnel and seen a woman, standing on the track, facing him. He had tried to stop but there hadn't been enough time. He was terribly upset and I felt sorry for him.

I found myself uncontrollably angry with Penny—that she had done this to us. Hadn't she thought about how it was going to affect her daughters, her sister, me, the innocent train driver, even the guys who'd had to pick her off the train track?

The day after Penny died a letter from her arrived, addressed to me and the girls. It apologized for the pain she had caused us, but said that we would be better off without her. "Don't mourn my going," she wrote. "I'm not worth it. But remember I love you all very much but you'll be better off without me."

How could she ever think that? We needed her, we loved her. I was so confused. At least twenty times a day I'd think if only I'd done this, if only I'd said that. I lived in guilt, and would not have been surprised if I'd been arrested for failing to see that my wife was mentally ill. Rationally I knew it wasn't possible, but I'd almost have felt better if it had happened. I felt like a worthless husband who had driven his wife to suicide.

I was like that for months. Even now, five years later, I think how different things might have been. After a few months I thought that if I couldn't talk about how I felt, I was going to explode. At home I was trying to be strong for the girls, at work I was trying to bury myself; but inside, there was a seething mass of rage and hate and guilt.

One night I had a dream. Penny was drowning in a river and I was standing on the bank, watching her. When she called to me, I shouted, "Help yourself!" I turned my back on her and walked away. I didn't need to be Sigmund Freud to recognize that dream's meaning.

When I realized how much I needed to talk, my employers arranged for me to see a psychiatrist for a few sessions. She was really helpful and explained to me that, from what I had told her about Penny and those last few months, there was no doubt that my wife had been severely depressed. The psychiatrist added that people who have been depressed and have had suicidal thoughts, but are regaining their energy, can be in danger. They may start to have the strength to accomplish what they couldn't when they felt weaker.

In those few sessions I cried, I ranted. I still couldn't believe or accept that Penny had taken her life. She had so much going for her, so much to live for. And knowing what she did about losing parents as a teenager, how could she have done it deliberately to the girls? I told the psychiatrist all of this. She suggested that it was the depression that had led Penny to commit suicide, and not Penny herself.

That's all very well. But you know, if I had seen how mentally ill she was, I'd have gotten her the help she needed. Instead, five years later, I can still wake up in the morning feeling guilty that I let my wife die. I might as well have pushed her under that train.

The girls? They grew up quick. They knew the truth, and they seem better at accepting that their mother was ill than I do. Leila told me that she knows her mother must have been really, really desperate, and so she doesn't blame her. I'm not saying that my daughters didn't have problems at the time. They did. There were nightmares, tantrums, lots of sore tummies or headaches. But we pulled through together.

For a long time I feared that people were avoiding me because they thought that in some way I'd been so awful to Penny that I'd driven her to it. But now I realize that they just felt awkward and didn't know what to do. The best support I got was from our next door neighbor. She would do the wash, cook meals, help out with the shopping. Then, when we all began to perk up a bit, she showed the girls some ideas for cooking.

Apart from the guilt, which I think will always remain with me, the worst thing is the loneliness. Nobody else I know who's my age has lost his wife. One or two are divorced, but that's different. I sit in, night after night, watching the girls do their homework or just watching television. My parents would like me to marry again, but I'm scared to get close to another woman. I feel I'm jinxed and would only bring her bad luck. I couldn't bear it if I married again and somehow lost my wife.

My parents won't ever talk about Penny. Soon after she died they told me they had always noticed something a "bit odd" about her, and that they had been disappointed when I announced we were going to get married. I was furious! This was the first I'd heard of this. I remember my mother's reaction very well. She'd been delighted, and enjoyed telling her friends "what a nice girl" her son Steve was marrying.

We then had a huge blow-up. They trashed Penny, saying what a terrible wife she had been, and how typically selfish it was of her to kill herself just because she was feeling "down." They couldn't accept depression as a clinical condition and discounted it as psychiatrists creating work for themselves.

We were all sitting around the table at the time. I asked Leila and her sister to leave the room, and then launched into a terrible tirade. I don't want to remember some of the things I called my parents, and in the end I walked out and went to a bar. Sitting there, staring at the bottle, I realized how difficult they must have found it to admit that their daughter-in-law had committed suicide. It was easier to dismiss her as "no good" than to accept that the Penny they had really liked had killed herself. It's not exactly what you brag about to the neighbors!

We made up soon after that dreadful day, but we didn't talk about Penny again. I know they haven't forgiven her for what she did to me and the girls. Actually, deep down, I'm not sure I have. Mostly it's the guilt I feel, but sometimes I feel so angry at what's happened to us as a family that it scares me.

<hr />

How can somebody like Steven ever grow beyond the confused emotions caused by the suicide of someone he loved? Many people in similar situations have turned to long-term counseling. There they can begin to understand better what is going on inside and gradually come to terms with the loss for which, to some degree, they feel responsible.

With suicide, the guilt can be more paralyzing than in any other bereavement. Somehow, though, it's essential to let it go—a seemingly simple act that is very difficult to achieve. Although one life has already been cut short, is it worth ruining those that remain? In Steven's case he had the reassurance that his wife was mentally ill. Some people whose relatives commit suicide don't always have that reassurance. There may have been no warning signs at all. What prompted the suicide may never be completely known: money troubles, extramarital relationships, overwhelming stress.

There is also the tragedy of a young person who commits suicide. In America, suicide is the third highest cause of death among young men in their teens or early twenties. In Britain, suicide is the third cause of death in all young adults, and the trend is getting worse. Not all of these young people set out to kill themselves, but their attempts were more cries for help—cries of help that went desperately wrong and were not heard until it was too late. Knowing that the young person did not intend suicide is no real consolation. The guilt still remains. "Why didn't I notice how unhappy she was?" "Why couldn't I tell how worried he was?" And added to that is the thought, "If only I had returned sooner, I might have arrived before it was too late."

Suicides are such tragic deaths, full of ambivalence and the endless "if only." The people involved may have little understanding or sympathy, and the bereaved are left behind—isolated by taboo and incomprehension, and racked by conflicting and confusing emotions. Is there any way through the difficult times ahead?

It is important not to assign blame. The normal human reaction to scapegoat is misplaced here. Transferring one's uneasy sense of personal responsibility to someone else is a psychological defense mechanism. In the aftermath of a suicide, anger could be directed toward almost everyone: police, doctors, other family members, self, and the person who has died. Blaming forces the internal spiral of guilt and resentment to destroy the very relationships that should sustain us at this traumatic time.

Steven's relationship with his parents almost collapsed after the catastrophic self-destruction of suicide. It is crucial instead to try to maintain relationships in which support and sharing the pain can take place.

Although suicide has not been regarded as a criminal act for a long time, there is still a stigma attached to it. There is acute sensitivity to the looks and thoughts of people outside the family, fear of judgment and blame. Sadly, the reactions of outsiders can cause a person to have even more anger and guilt. "Let them mind their own business," we snap. And then we think, "Maybe they've got a point." We need to face these contradictory feelings and work through the pain and horror, confronting them rather than ignoring them. Only then will they ease.

The first step to coming to terms with our feelings is to find a good listener: a professional counselor, health visitor, doctor, or pastoral minister. It could be a good friend—though that person, too, may need support. Whoever we turn to, we need to talk it all out, if necessary going over the same ground again and again. We need someone who won't judge, who won't try to deny our feelings, and who will listen not just once but many times.

Some people bereaved by suicide encounter the supposedly well-meaning friend, who says, "Well, he meant to kill himself, so there's no need to grieve. He wanted to die!" This is the classic attitude of those who want to distance themselves from pain and to deny the feelings of all who are left grieving. They feel better by saying what they do, but the recipient doesn't. The key thing to remember is, "Even if the person I loved wanted to die, I didn't want her to die. That's why I have every right to mourn."

For Christians a suicide may be particularly hard to accept. Biblical teaching holds that life is a sacred gift from God and not to be ended by human hands. So there may be enormous concern and fear that someone who has committed suicide is now in outer darkness or somehow banished from God's love. The Church itself at one time prohibited those who died by suicide from being buried in consecrated ground, but that is no longer the case. The revised Order of Christian Funerals includes prayers for those who have died by suicide.

As Christians we really need to fix our eyes upon God. For in God we see love as the prime mover. God knows and shares our pain and brings us healing. If, in the deepest depression and mental illness, in great anxiety or overwhelming stress, someone loses sight of the way to go on, God's infinite mercy embraces that person so much the more.

Taboo Deaths

❖ "Taboo deaths" reflect the more complex, less comfortable sides of human nature. Disturbing inner turmoil, confusion regarding sexuality, or thoughts of self-destruction are often things we try to ignore. They can be unnerving.

❖ The strength of feeling that leads to willful self-destruction seems to stray beyond society's norm. The bereaved can find themselves socially isolated. The pain they suffer is an unwelcome reminder of the unknown depth of human complexity. Society and the people who make up society tend to recoil from the shadow side of life. Sometimes isn't it easier to condemn than it is to try to understand?

Everyone Can Feel Loss
Be Wary of Exclusion

All my life I've felt that my mother didn't really die. I'm seventy now, and my mother died when I was six. I didn't go to her funeral, and nobody ever really talked about her again. I used to think that she had run away. Even now, though I've seen her grave, it still doesn't seem real.

———◆◆◆———

I couldn't bring myself to tell our four-year-old, Helen, that her baby sister had died in the hospital. We didn't think she was old enough to understand; we just said Sophie had gone away. But we really struggled with Helen. Her behavior was terrible, she wouldn't settle down at night, and she started to wet the bed again. The social worker said Helen was grieving for her sister.

———◆◆◆———

People think my son Paul is "not with it." He suffered brain damage when he was born. Now he's twenty and goes to adult day care for people with learning disabilities. When his father died, Paul sensed how sad I was and came and held me. I explained about his dad's death, and he joined me at the funeral parlor. Paul cried and knew only too well what the death of his father meant.

There are a lot of opinions about how much information children should be told about death. There are parents who feel that their children should be protected at all costs from any notion of death or dying. Others believe that from a very early age children are able to feel loss, and the cause of that loss needs to be honestly, but gently, explained.

Loss is also felt by children and adults with learning disabilities and older adults affected by dementia, Alzheimer's disease, or other psycho-social conditions. A person who seems inarticulate or confused, or who doesn't seem to be what we might unfeelingly call "normal," can still feel the loss of a relationship. Any person may feel loss, even a person with altered consciousness.

The first time I encountered people with learning disabilities, I was terrified. The visit was part of a community involvement program to widen our experience of life beyond school. It certainly did that, and over the weeks we visited, my terror left. I soon realized the enormous capacity for love and affection shown by people who were born with learning difficulties or who later develop them. This love and affection isn't always expressed in the usual way. It's often more poignant and meaningful than that.

Some years after that experience at school, I was involved in making several television programs with the l'Arche communities. Through the various encounters, and particularly through the deep spirituality there, I have come to realize how wrong it is to dismiss people with learning disabilities. Their feelings, emotions, and their capacity for love and loss are just as great as anyone else's.

This chapter therefore discusses how best to deal with bereavement in children, people with learning disabilities, and the confused elderly.

Children

Children perceive so much from the attitudes and behavior of the people around them. If they are excluded from bereavement on the grounds that it is too distressing for them to be told the truth, they will still notice the distress of the adults. Puzzled by what is going on around them and sensing they've been excluded from something terrible, they begin to form the attitude that death is a taboo subject and not to be talked about as part of everyday conversation. Sadly, it will also mean that the child is poorly prepared for grief. He or she may carry that attitude into adulthood.

The same attitude may also incorporate some unnecessary guilt. Young children see themselves as being at the center of their world. In the event of a death close to them, it is common for children to believe they are at fault. Many even think that they have somehow killed the person they love (or hate) and that they have caused the whole sequence of events. Not so long ago, one child in a foster home was heard to say in his goodnight prayers, "Dear God, please tell Mommy that when I killed her it wasn't my fault." The mother of the child in question had died in a car crash, and the child had been nowhere near the scene.

How do we prevent such ideas from forming? How does one begin to explain to a child what death is? If the child has lost a parent or someone else close to him or her, how can the child be helped through the grief he or she will be feeling? These are hard issues to address, especially if the person closest to the bereaved child is suffering the same loss and is, therefore, not prepared to handle another person's feelings.

If at all possible, the key is to acknowledge the shared loss and to grieve together. We must mourn together where possible, and deal honestly and gently with the child concerned.

Shirley's story

Shirley's husband, Roy, was diagnosed as having liver cancer when their two children were aged nine and six. Tests had shown that Roy's cancer was beyond treatment and nothing could be done except to relieve the pain. The doctors thought that he only had a very short time left to live.

Both Shirley and Roy wanted him to be at home when he died, so Roy was released from the hospital. Their children, Alice and Daniel, only knew that their father wasn't well. Although both parents wanted them to know about the cancer, the question was how to tell them.

For the first few days that Roy was at home we said nothing to the kids. They just knew that "Daddy was still feeling poorly." But other family members knew and, of course, came to visit. Roy's parents were still alive and deeply upset by the news, as were close friends. When Roy had gone into the hospital, he had never dreamt that he was so seriously ill. But it reached the point where something had to be said to the children. Sooner or later they would hear something or sense that something was terribly wrong.

The amazing thing was that before we had decided what to say, Alice, our older child, just came right out with it.

One afternoon she was sitting on Roy's knee watching TV while I was out shopping with Dan. Apparently she had asked her dad how sick he really was. Roy asked her why she had asked that. She said, "Because everyone who comes to the house is now sad." She noted that these people were also being really nice to her and Daniel, which she said was "kind of weird!"

Alice is very observant, and she was probably picking up on our apprehension. When Roy told her he was feeling pretty poorly, Alice quite simply asked him if he was going to die.

I think that until then, Roy had found it hard enough to admit it to himself, let alone to our nine-year-old daughter. But he just said yes, he was going to die. And soon. He said that of course he didn't want to leave us all, but that he had cancer and that the doctors couldn't make him better. He was very good with her, very honest. He said he was going to get more and more sick and not be able to do things he liked anymore. Alice just took it all in and understood.

When Dan and I returned, we found them in tears, cuddling one another. I knew at once what had happened, so then I told Dan. It was hard, and all I could say was, "Dan, we're all crying because Daddy is very, very sick. He's not going to get better. He's going to die soon."

Dan just looked confused and puzzled, so I picked him up and we joined Roy and Alice on the couch. Dan asked if he could go with Roy when he died. He was so sweet and concerned. Roy replied, "Dan, that's a really nice thought. It would be good to have company, but I've got to die on my own. You've got lots of years in front of you to live here with Mommy and Alice."

And then came the question, "But what do you do when you're dead?" I groaned inwardly—honestly, the capacity of children to ask the questions everyone would love to know the answers to! Roy was wonderful, and said, "I don't know what I'll do when I'm dead, Dan; that's the mystery. But I'll find out soon. I'm not frightened by it, though. And I'm sure I'm going to heaven and that I'll meet my Granny and Grandad there, and I hope I'll see Jesus, too."

It's odd, but though it was agonizing to tell the children that Roy was dying, we also felt great relief. Everything was out in the open, and the children were free to ask or say whatever they wanted to.

We almost enjoyed the next few days together. Dan and Alice spent a lot of time with Roy, playing games, reading, or just laying on the bed with him, watching TV. But it was soon obvious that Roy was deteriorating. The doctor increased his pain medication and the nurses began visiting more. Roy started to spend more and more time sleeping.

I was really worried about what to do with Dan and Alice. I wondered if they should go and stay with my mom to spare them the pain of watching Roy die. But I wasn't sure. Eventually a good friend of mine, Mandy, offered to come and live with us. She had always gotten along with the children, and it seemed to be the best solution. I could spend time with Roy without worrying about Alice and Dan, and looking after them. And the kids were able to be with their father when they wanted.

One sad thing was seeing Roy's parents age so much—almost overnight. They came as often as they could, but they'd taken a terrible blow. Only about a week after Mandy moved in, the doctor said she didn't think Roy would be conscious much longer.

I remember one day when Dan was playing on the floor of his father's room. Very soon Alice came racing in from school, making a beeline for Roy. This had become the pattern ever since they had known how ill he was. Roy enjoyed it, and the children had chosen it.

I just about managed to talk to both of them during their snack that day. I explained that the doctor had said that Daddy was going to die very soon now, and that what would happen next would be that he would go into a deep sleep. He wouldn't wake up again, and maybe tonight when they kissed Daddy goodnight they might like to give him a special kiss.

Roy knew it wouldn't be long, too. He wanted his painkilling injections to be delayed somewhat, so that he would be more alert during his time with Dan and Alice. It was a very special time for all of us. Roy gave each of the kids a photograph album that he had put together, so that when they were older they would have something to remember their dad by.

By the time Roy's parents arrived, Dan was already in bed. Alice asked if she could stay up and of course I said yes. Roy was sort of drifting in and out of sleep. I tried to reassure him, saying everything was fine, and that we loved him.

By midnight Alice was hardly able to keep her eyes open, bless her. So she gave Roy a kiss, and I put her to bed. Then there were just the three of us—Roy's parents and me—watching and waiting. During the night, his breathing became more and more labored, and by dawn I began to fear that each breath would be his last. I spoke gently, saying it was all right and that he could go now. But inside I felt panic. How on earth would we cope on our own? At the same time, I felt as if I were in a dream, and that soon I'd wake up and everything would be back to normal. I couldn't quite believe that Roy really was dying.

Roy died at 6:30 that morning. His parents went into the living room to leave me alone. Dan was the first one up. He poked his head around the door and knew, without my saying anything. He just hugged me silently, looked at his dad and kissed him.

Then Alice came, and do you know what she said? She was upset, but all she said was, "Daddy will be happy now. He was so sick, and he won't hurt now, will he?" Then she sat by him, crying softly. She didn't stay long. When we left to join the others in the kitchen, she said, "That didn't really look like Daddy. He looked different!"

I felt relieved that Alice and Dan were there to share this with me. I was really shaken. Although I'd had time to prepare for Roy's death, nothing really prepares you for the raw finality of it. Maybe it was selfish to have the children there, but I felt that it was also right that they should have had the chance to say goodbye.

The next hurdle was the funeral. I couldn't imagine how I was going to get through it on my own, let alone with the children. They had been so much a part of all that we'd been through and I asked if they wanted to come. Of course they did! Mandy was there as well. We explained what would happen and tried to prepare them as much as we could. I didn't want it to be too distressing for them.

That was two years ago. Sometimes one of the children will ask why Roy died, and I have to say to them, "I just don't know!" I didn't want to say things to them like, "Well, God wanted Daddy to go and live with him now," because I can't accept that, so I don't see why they should. They go to church and to Sunday school religious ed; and they say their prayers every night. But I feel it's wrong to lead them to think of God as deliberately taking their daddy from them.

I'm glad that they remained in the house and didn't go to my mother's that night. I'd lost my husband and they'd lost their father. It had meant so much to Roy to have them with him. When he knew they were due back from school he always made an effort to look presentable. And I think being there helped the children understand all that happened. They saw how sick their father was, and I think they saw that death needn't be frightening.

They still talk about Roy a lot—sometimes just wishing he was around. For Father's Day we go to visit Roy's grave and leave fresh flowers there. It's hard when the kids at school are talking about Father's Day, and my two are reminded that they no longer have their dad. Obviously there are children in their school whose parents are divorced, but most of them still see their fathers. So if the younger ones make cards for their dads, Dan makes his for his grandpa.

I went to see Dan and Alice's teachers when Roy was first diagnosed, and made sure they knew, too, when Roy had died. The teachers seemed grateful. Alice's teacher explained to the class what had happened while Alice was away those few days around the funeral. I also informed the teachers what we had told the children, asking them to use the same response when Dan or Alice questioned them. I didn't want the children to be given different versions about death. We had tried to be as honest as we could. If we didn't know something, we said so. And that's been my attitude through these last two years. If I'm feeling depressed and they notice, I'll say that I'm missing their daddy. If they want answers to questions that even adults can't answer, I'll admit that I don't know. I've come to realize more and more that it's best to be honest with children, accepting the limits to their comprehension, then that's the best thing to do. It's tough, but sometimes it's a tough world.

◆◦◆◦◆

I've told the story of Shirley and Roy at some length because it shows how a family can tackle the issue of bereavement in children. It also shows what a great deal of strength children can share with adults.

Think what the alternative might have been if they had been sent away to their grandparents', occasionally visiting Daddy at home, and finally being told, "Daddy has gone away."

Children can get stuck in their grief in the same way that adults can, if the experience is handled badly. Emotional development and educational progress can suddenly cease or go backward, and even mechanical skills of coordination or managing daily routines can be affected. Years later, the suppressed grief will eventually show itself in different forms, such as passive aggression, phobias, playing life's "victim," or deeply rebellious behavior.

Fortunately the death of a parent is comparatively rare. But children will still encounter death. Their grandparents, teachers, neighbors, or even a school friend may die. Shirley's account of trying to be open and honest with her children applies to these circumstances too.

Children also lose pets—hamsters, cats, dogs—in the course of their childhood. In all of these occasions, children can begin to understand death. Simple funeral services for animals (with a burial in the garden or back yard), conducted by the children themselves, can be both moving and comical. Yet they provide an opportunity to grieve and to begin to accept the loss of a much-loved companion.

Death cannot be hidden from children. They see it on the TV, and it's the stuff of their play: "Bang! Bang!

You're dead!" Use opportunities as they occur to talk openly and honestly about death.

Learning disabilities

Twenty years ago, Kate and Robert thought that they would never be able to have a child of their own. Then, when Kate was almost forty, she discovered that she was pregnant. Delighted, she and Robert planned for the arrival of their baby.

When Polly was born, however, the hospital staff were restrained. A consultant was summoned and Polly was rushed away. Neither Kate nor Robert were allowed to hold her, and they were told their baby daughter was very ill.

Polly pulled through, as Kate and Robert kept an anxious vigil by her crib. One day they were called in to talk with the consultant. Gently they were told that Polly may have suffered brain damage. She also had Down's Syndrome, and had little chance of a normal life.

Normal! Normal! What's normal? People are so ready to write off those they consider to be different. Polly was our daughter, and Robert and I intended to look after her no matter how disabled she was.

Polly came home to live with us. She was a beautiful child: happy, full of fun, and affectionate. Even now, so many years later, she never says more than a few words, but she doesn't have to say, "I love you." When she throws her arms around me and gives me a great big kiss, I know she loves me—and I love her, too.

Then last year, when Polly was nineteen, Robert died. He was riding his motorcycle home when a car hit him. The driver never stopped. Robert was taken to the hospital, unconscious and in critical condition. He never regained consciousness and died two days later.

When I first heard of Robert's accident, Polly was out at a crafts and activities club. I asked a good friend, Phil, to meet her and bring her to his family. "Tell Polly I've gone shopping," I said. Then I raced to the hospital and discovered how critically ill Robert was. I was absolutely distraught. Time just stopped as I sat there, begging him to live.

I have no idea how much later it was before a nurse came to me, saying that somebody named Phil insisted that he had to talk to me. Phil?

Polly! How could I forget her! Phil told me that she wouldn't settle down. She was huddled in a corner of the room, banging her head on the wall. He said Polly was really disturbed, and he just didn't know what to do for her—bring her to the hospital or call a doctor for advice?

My gut feeling told me to have her brought to the hospital. Robert was so ill, and maybe seeing him would help Polly. We had never talked to her about death, and I wasn't at all sure how she would respond now. But somehow Phil had to warn her. It wouldn't be fair for her to see Robert without knowing he was critically injured. I told Phil to tell Polly that her dad was very sick and to clutch his stomach. She would understand that.

As soon as he did that, Polly began to calm down. In no time at all, they were at the hospital and we met at the intensive care unit. Polly rushed to hug me, and cried. An understanding nurse clasped one of Polly's hands and I held the other as we walked with her into the room where Robert was. She stood still, looking intently at the bed. For a second I thought I'd made a mistake, but then she moved forward and gently touched Robert's hand. She looked puzzled that he didn't respond, and touched him again, harder this time.

I began to cry then, uncontrollably. I couldn't be strong any longer. As the nurse tried to comfort me, a huge bear hug grabbed me. Polly's hugs are unique, and I recognized her embrace immediately. We cried together. She understood how sick Robert was.

On the day Robert died, I was alone with him and had time to say my own goodbyes. Polly was back with Phil and his family, although she'd been at the hospital several times. Each time she had been very quiet and studied Robert closely. Now she returned to see him in death.

He looked at rest. A bandage covered his battered head, but the tubes and intensive care machines were gone. Polly came in, looked, and touched. I told her Robert had died. There was no way I could explain to her what that meant, but she touched Robert again, and then slowly began to stroke his face. Her voice made the noises which she makes when she's unhappy. On and on they went, and I could do nothing to ease her pain. I cried again. "It's just you and me now, Polly," I said as we left the hospital together.

That night she slept in the bed beside me. Polly slept heavily and I dozed, thankful for her warmth yet at the same time longing for that warmth to be Robert. The next morning, as people began to call the house, Polly wouldn't leave my side. She held my hand until it hurt, and with her other hand she clutched one of Robert's sweaters. She knew that Robert had gone, and was scared that I might go too.

Over the next few weeks Polly sensed my own pain. She was very gentle and stroked me a lot. When she found me in tears she would rock me from side to side, as a mother does with a baby. I very much wanted Polly to be a part of Robert's funeral, so Polly helped the pastor light four candles around the coffin. When he told the congregation that the candles were for Robert, Polly's dad, Polly nodded wisely. At the end of the service, after the coffin had disappeared behind the curtains of the crematorium, Polly blew the candles out.

As I walked through my grief, and struggled to survive without Robert, I know that Polly grieved too. She didn't have the words to say what she was feeling, but I knew she missed her dad. To this day I'm glad that Phil phoned the hospital and risked disturbing my private time. Afterward he told me how he almost hadn't called, but he just felt sure—seeing how disturbed Polly was—that somehow she knew something terrible had happened. She needed to see Robert, in the same way that any other child would want to see her dad. I'm glad she came, that I hadn't excluded her in the mistaken belief that she wouldn't understand, and that we were able to share the grief we both felt with Robert's death.

Old age

Although this next account relates to the particular circumstance of old age, it could well have happened to a younger person suffering from Alzheimer's disease (pre-senile dementia), or from any mental condition that produces confusion, loss of memory, or unpredictable behavior. Even if we think a person has no understanding that a loved one has died, we can never be certain. Most of the evidence shows that we would be wrong.

Peggy and Arnold's story

Every day since Peggy was admitted to a nursing home after a severe stroke, her husband Arnold walked up the hill to visit her. They had been married for sixty years, and he was devoted to her. He didn't always stay a long time, but would sit beside Peggy, holding her hand and talking to her. Peggy's stroke had robbed her of speech, and she seemed to have difficulty understanding what was said to her. Her left side was paralyzed, and she was confined to bed. Sometimes she would get confused and upset, and the nursing staff wondered if Peggy really knew where she was. But when Arnold sat beside her, her eyes met his and she always seemed to recognize him.

Then, one day, Arnold didn't come to the nursing home. Nobody had heard from him and the staff was concerned. The local pastor tells the story:

I'd come to know Arnold and Peggy well. I had enormous admiration for the way Arnold visited Peggy day in, day out. A couple of times I was with Peggy when he arrived, and her eyes would just light up when she saw him.

When I heard that he hadn't visited that day, I was concerned and went over to his home. The milk was on the doorstep, the curtains were drawn. There was no reply when I shouted through the letterbox, so I called the police.

Arnold was dead. He was in bed, in his pajamas, as if he'd died peacefully in his sleep. For Arnold there would be no more daily walks up that steep hill to the nursing home. But Peggy? Would she understand that Arnold had died? She was terribly confused; it was only when she saw Arnold that something seemed to register.

Heading back to the nursing home, I wondered how to tell Peggy. Maybe I shouldn't even try. Would she notice that Arnold wasn't visiting anymore? Yet she deserved to be treated with dignity and respect. Who was I to judge what Peggy may or may not understand? Her husband had died, and I would try to tell her.

As I approached Peggy's bed, her eyes opened and then closed as soon as she saw me. Although I had sat with Peggy many times, she never recognized me the next time. She seemed to know Arnold, and Arnold alone.

I called Peggy's name several times, and eventually she opened her eyes, looking blankly at me. I introduced myself again, took her hand, and then asked, "Are you waiting for Arnold, Peggy?" This time there was a flicker of interest. So, as gently as I could, I told Peggy that Arnold had died.

She stared right through me. I tried again, this time taking the photo of Arnold which sat on her dresser. One solitary tear formed and ran slowly down her cheek. Her good hand tightened around mine, and I knew that Peggy understood. I said a prayer, and as I did so, her grip slackened. Peggy dropped off to sleep.

Within twenty-four hours, Peggy also died—as if Arnold had been her reason for hanging on to life. Knowing that he was gone, she gave up the fight.

<hr />

We know so little about human brain functioning. Someone may appear to have no recognition, or to live in a confused state, but we cannot be certain how much information a person is able to take in. In the event of the death of someone close, it is important to find ways of telling the bereaved person and helping him or her to grieve.

If a person is too ill to attend a funeral service, a hospital chaplain can hold a service at the person's bedside during the funeral. In this way, the ill person feels included. The service may be an important part of recognizing the reality of the death.

Everyone can feel loss

Although all of the accounts in this chapter relate to circumstances that are relatively rare, there are truths for all of us.

❖ We all feel loss—adults, children, people with learning disabilities, the confused elderly. No one is an exception. We might try to protect ourselves or others from the pain of that loss, but grief remains the price we pay for loving. We may try to hide or suppress our grief, but sooner or later it will emerge.

❖ We cannot assume that others will not feel or understand their loss. We may want to protect them from pain or spare them suffering, but human beings glean information in more ways than words. Our desire to protect another may only cause confusion and anxiety as the person senses that something is wrong.

❖ Everyone has the right to know the truth. The truth needs to be told—with sensitivity, compassion, and, above all, love.

Putting the Pieces Back
Together Again
Can We?

Meeting with other parents who also lost a child is what helps me most. I know it sounds morbid, but it isn't. Our small group meets every month so people feel free to talk or to cry. Having the chance to say how things have gone means so much to me.

Soon after Joe, my husband, died, I asked my daughter to clear out all his belongings. I couldn't bear to see them around the house. Now I wish I hadn't done that; I have so little to remind me of him. Fortunately my daughter kept some of his drawings and books. She was confident that in time I'd appreciate them. At least I've got those.

My nighttime strategy was this: I bought a portable television for the bedroom. Every night I went to bed armed with a good book, a thermos of decaf coffee and something to munch—say some cookies or an apple. Sometimes I didn't need them, but more often than not I'd wake in the night. Then, when I felt ready, I'd fall asleep again.

It's been said before in this book, but it's important to repeat a previous point: grief needs to be faced and lived through. Despite the "useful" strategy of numbing or denying the pain we feel, there is a danger if we just force the feelings underground.

There are, however, ways in which we can make it easier for ourselves to live through the pain. Much of what follows in this chapter is based on the experience of people who have found things that either worked for them or that didn't work.

Numbing the pain

Tranquilizers, sleeping pills, and antidepressants are all commonly prescribed drugs for people who are newly bereaved. Another drug that people often use is alcohol. The trouble with all of these is that they only mask the pain. It might seem that they are "making the pain go away," but the effect is only temporary and "anesthetic." When the effect wears off, the pain returns.

A temporary "break" may be helpful, but the problem develops when "temporary" becomes permanent. A glass or two of one's favorite liquor can help someone relax, unless the doctor has prescribed a conflicting medication. But regular, heavy drinking, or deliberate drinking in order to forget the grief, is dangerous. The person concerned needs to talk to someone about that grief and all that he or she is feeling or, perhaps, trying *not* to feel.

Similarly, taking a sleeping pill to break one's pattern of insomnia won't harm anyone and may even be of great help. But using pills night after night can lead to dependency. Those who have tried to stop a habit of tranquilizers testify that it is extremely painful.

Tranquilizers and antidepressants are different. Tranquilizers have an almost immediate effect, whereas antidepressants begin to work in the body after building up for a period of about two weeks. In cases of genuine clinical depression, antidepressants have a useful role to play, but sadness after a death does not necessarily lead to clinical depression. Mourning is a normal human response to loss. To mourn is not the same thing as being depressed, but prolonged mourning can lead to, or be a sign of, depression.

Many people casually report feeling depressed, but they probably mean that they're fed up. The illness of depression is much more than that. A doctor diagnoses clinical depression and prescribes antidepressants when the body needs them; and no one should worry about taking them.

Tranquilizers, on the other hand, may well be prescribed for the newly bereaved because they work quickly and at times their short-term use is appropriate. However, tranquilizers are addictive over a longer period, and they also cause trouble in the future by blocking the grief within.

Geraldine's story

My husband's death came like a bolt from the blue when I was fifty-one years old. It was a tremendous shock. My doctor prescribed some tranquilizers, and I felt they helped. So I asked for some more, and when they came to an end I tried coping without them. But I felt so awful that I asked if I could renew my prescription. My physician said nothing about addiction and happily wrote out another prescription.

About five years later I was forced to face the issue when I saw a television program about addiction. A woman described how she'd been trying to stop taking tranquilizers and what a tremendous struggle that had been. "I don't have a problem," I reassured myself, and decided to prove it.

It was terrible! Panic attacks, agoraphobia, insomnia, shaking, sweating, fearful anxiety. I became a complete mess. Only the support of friends, family, and the professional help of a psychiatrist saw me through it. Now I realize that, while I thought I was successfully blocking the pain that Frank's death had caused me, I was hiding from it. Besides facing some of that, I also had to cope with the withdrawal symptoms.

My advice to anyone using tranquilizers to deaden their grief is to reduce them under medical supervision. Hopefully the person will not become addicted, and life is eventually better without them. Looking back, I might as well have been a robot for the five years I took the tranquilizers.

Moving house

One of the biggest decisions to be faced by new widows or widowers is what to do with their home. Some want to stay in the place they feel closest to the person who died. Others want the complete opposite: the home becomes too painful a reminder of the past, and they want to rid themselves of it as soon as possible.

Sometimes there is no choice in the matter. A move is forced on them because of finances, legal disputes, and bills. In addition to the loss of a partner, there is also loss of the security that one's home represented.

Even when there is a choice, there are probably good, practical reasons to move. Financially it can make sense and be easier having a smaller home. The key point, however, is to take time before coming to any decision. The first year after the death of a partner can be an emotional roller-coaster. What someone feels at three months is not necessarily what the person will feel a year later. Unless there are pressing reasons to move, it is better to remain until a long-term decision can be made—one based on what honors the future, rather than what feels good in the heat of the moment.

Ruth's story

Ruth was sixty-three when her husband, Larry, died at home after a three-year illness. They had been married for forty years and had two daughters who had moved into their own homes some years before. Ruth stayed for eighteen months in the house she and Larry had lived in for the last thirty-five years. Then she put the house on the market and was able to buy a condo in the same neighborhood.

It would have been crazy to move anywhere else. I have some really good friends here; and it's a place I love and feel safe in. But the family home was just too big for me. To be truthful, it had been too big for just Larry and me after the girls left home. But it was a lovely house, and neither of us really wanted to move. When Larry died, I had to look at the future. A time will come when I'm not as strong as I am now; and I need a place that I can look after easily.

For the first eighteen months after Larry's death I needed to be in the house. It held so many memories. Right after his death I went to live with one of my daughters, but I think that was a mistake. Everything was unfamiliar. Don't get me wrong—it was nice to be pampered and cared for, but it was a different bed, a different house, and her daily life was different. I felt in the way. So when I did go back to my own home—although I was dreading being on my own there—it was where I needed to be. It was so reassuring to hear the old central heating system clanking along through the evening, and to have all sorts of things that reminded me of Larry around the place: his clothes, his books, his treasured pipes.

When I decided to move, I was amazed at the girls' reaction. They hadn't lived there for at least eight years, but neither of them wanted me to sell. They kept telling me I'd regret it; that it was too soon. But I knew the time was right. My life now was as a single person, and that house was too big. Also, I'd said my goodbyes to Larry. I still missed him, but it was time for me to move on.

Eventually I was able to have a long discussion with my daughters. Their advice not to sell had more to do with the fact that they didn't want me to sell! Neither of them had completed their own grieving for their father. As long as the family house remained, they could almost convince themselves that life hadn't really changed since their father had died. That weekend, as they helped me move, they realized what they had been doing. Although we cried a lot for a few days, it was good. We had dinner together on the last night, perched on packing cases—Chinese take-out and champagne! I raised my glass and toasted Larry. Something like, "Larry thank you. You were a great husband, a loving dad, and this house meant so much. Be at rest!"

Well, I've always been one for drama. It marked the end of an era, and it seemed right to do it. The next day, I moved. Sometimes I think Larry would have hated this condo, but I have to remind myself that this is my home. Everything's very feminine, particularly my bedroom! It's manageable, it's pretty, and it's home!

Ruth is eager to live independently as long as she can. Many people at her age would probably want to do something similar. But she remembers a widower in the neighborhood, a little older than herself, who moved in with his son and daughter-in-law for good.

It was tragic. He aged so quickly and seemed to lose his confidence. People said that he never recovered from losing his wife. I'm sure that to some extent that's because he lost some of himself when he moved in with his son. They only live five miles away, but he gave up coming over to bowl. He used to be so involved in the local church, but soon gave that up as well. He became very dependent on his son, and—although it all happened for the best of motives—I can't help thinking that it was the wrong thing to do. He seemed to lose all interest in living, and only nine months later he died in his sleep one night.

Home is so important and basic to life that it is worth the time and effort to make a good decision, not rush one way or the other until it's clear what is best. Someone who is rushing to make changes about where he or she lives needs to pause and ask what the rush is all about. Undue haste may overlook some implications, and feelings of grief can cloud decision-making. It really is better to have as little change as possible during the first year.

The rest of our life lies ahead of us, however long or short that may be. Bereavement is one of the greatest stresses a human being will ever face. It's important to give the future a good start; and a lot of that future will be influenced by the choice of where to live.

If after a year or so one is still undecided about what to do, he or she could usefully consider what one's wishes might be in the future. How old is the person? What is his or her health like? Is the home the person lives in at the moment too big to cope with now, or will it be too big in five years? Where do most of the person's friends live? Where are the activities he or she takes part in now, or might in the future? How would he or she feel about leaving this current home? What are the advantages to staying? How does the person feel about moving?

Of course, it may be that a person finally decides the best plan would be to simply stay where they are. If so, then fine. He or she needs to remain and ignore any well-meant persuasion to move!

But what about the people who are forced by circumstances to move after a death, sometimes almost immediately? Perhaps they are suffering financial hardship. Here there is no opportunity to take time to think about what is best, no choice to move or not to move.

In such cases, it may be possible to "buy time" to allow the emotional turmoil to ease, after which a more permanent decision can be made.

Elsie's story

Elsie had lived all her adult life in homes that were tied to her husband's work. When Ken died, she had three months to move out.

At first I panicked. I didn't know where to start. Ken and I had never discussed what I'd do if he died first, and I'd always avoided thinking about it. We had no children, and although his pension would give some financial security, it certainly wouldn't cover a mortgage.

My friend, Belinda, stepped in to help. She took me down to the city housing department where they promised to help. But the waiting lists were long, even for people like me who were homeless. Homeless! I hated the phrase. That evening I sat up all night long, terrified about the future, and longing so much for Ken that I even thought about killing myself to be with him.

With Belinda's help I began to devise a plan for the future. She warned me against making rash decisions, and helped me find time to think and recover. We agreed that if I stayed in the area, some things at least would be familiar—shops, the church, and especially friends.

Belinda offered me a room in her house, but I wanted to be on my own. The sooner I learned to stand on my own two feet, the better! She helped me find an apartment near her. It was tiny, not very attractive. A lot of the furniture Ken and I had bought had to be sold. But my favorite things, the ones that held good memories of our life together, went into storage until I could sort out a more permanent option.

I stayed there for almost a year, but in the meantime found a seniors' housing development with an opening. It felt good to plan where I would put the furniture that was in storage. And I reached a stage where I was looking forward to moving again. This would be my permanent home, and that felt great!

Elsie was able to keep some of her options open until she could decide, in her own time, what she most wanted to do. If a quick move is required for any reason, it is important to try to find temporary solutions. Staying with friends, family, or even finding rented property like

Elsie did, can help. It's all about finding somewhere to stay, which isn't binding but which buys time.

It is, however, good to keep some things familiar. Bereavement is such an enormous change that we need some stability. People we know and who know us are vital. Where are the places and who are the people from whom we can draw comfort and support? What are the things in our homes that remind us now, and will remind us in the future, of the person we have loved? We need to keep them safe. At present they may only be a sad reminder of all that is lost, but in time we will treasure them for the good memories they hold.

Rebuilding a life

The relevance of this section will depend on the nature of one's bereavement. Much of what follows is related to surviving after the loss of a spouse, but, with a bit of adaptation, other elements apply to most major bereavements.

The key to rebuilding a life after losing someone close is to realize that no one will return to life as it was before. The change is irrevocable, and the journey through grief involves adapting to that change, not trying to pretend it hasn't happened.

If those who are now alone were caregivers for the person who died, time may weigh heavily on their hands. Before the death there was always something that needed to be done (the washing, changing the bedclothes, cooking), and they may have had people dropping by the house all day—not just friends and family, but visiting nurses, physicians, and pastoral ministers. Now, everything is quiet and they can't think what to do next.

Even without home care responsibilities, the time before the death became a very intense time. Normal daily routines may have been replaced by "living at the very heart of life itself." Acutely aware of the proximity of death, everyday concerns would have been forgotten in the face of the big issues of life and death.

Then came the death. There would have been a lot of activity, things to be done, arrangements to be made. And now? Nothing! All that's left is the future—alone. That can look very scary, especially if there has been a sense of living in that twilight existence created by coming close to the other world, the world of heaven and eternity. Everyday matters still seem irrelevant. Yet, in the weeks and months ahead, the grieving person needs to gradually adapt to normality in this world again.

Vivienne's story

Vivienne and her family were devastated by a death at the beginning of their summer vacation. She was forty-four when her husband died suddenly, leaving her with a son sixteen and a daughter eighteen. In September, Gemma, the daughter, was due to start her nurse's training at a hospital some 100 miles away.

Once the funeral was over and the various relatives had left, the three of us tiptoed around one another in the house. It felt wrong to have music blasting, or to quarrel, which had been common occurences before. I faced a dilemma. We had booked a family vacation in Spain for the last two weeks of August, only a few weeks away, and I just didn't know what to do.

The three of us talked about it and decided that we should still go. I was having terrible problems sleeping and kept dissolving in tears, but I was also concerned that the children would have something to look forward to. So, off we went. My first panic was having to drive the rental car from the airport. My husband had always done the driving because I hate it, but we survived long enough to arrive safely at the villa.

It was in a beautiful setting, close to the beach, and as we sat together on the patio and watched the sunset, I was glad we had come. There were a number of occasions in those two weeks when I thought the complete opposite, but the first night was fine. I managed to sleep well, but when I saw families together on the beach, I regretted going. We had a barbecue and the kids remembered that their dad was always the one to get it going, and when I caught a mysterious bug for about three days, I wished I was back in my own home.

But the trip did us good. When we returned, the music began to blare again and the house began to feel more like a home than a funeral parlor. It was then that Gemma announced that she wasn't going to start her nursing classes. I was appalled. Although I'd been dreading her leaving home for the first time—at this time of all times—I didn't want her life to be more damaged by her father's death than necessary.

It turned out that she didn't want to leave me alone with Paul. She felt that he wouldn't support me enough, and that I needed her around too. Paul and I were able to dissuade her about that, and so, a few days later with a sinking heart, I was driving my first-born to start her new life without me. I worried about how much change she could handle in such a short period of time, but I couldn't insulate her as she'd tried to do to me.

So in three months our family of four was cut in half. Now it was just Paul and me. He was very moody and touchy, and I don't think I was much better. But off he went to school, and I was left at home, day after day. I got to be very restless, cleaning furiously, and then I began to think about the future and felt very low. I was only forty-four. Was I going to spend the rest of my life as a housewife? Soon Paul would be heading off to college, and then what?

I knew that financially I was very lucky. Jim had always joked about how much he would be worth dead, and now I'd found out. Life insurance, endowment mortgages, pensions. As long as I wasn't wildly extravagant, I certainly had no financial worries in the future. But what to do with the rest of my life? The image of the Merry Widow wasn't quite me.

So, in the middle of all my grief at Jim's death, a little flame of hope for the future began to burn. Before the children were born I'd never had a career. I just worked my way through a variety of secretarial jobs until I met Jim and we fell in love. But now I wanted to work again. I didn't want to have to live off Jim's "death money," as I saw it, for the rest of my life.

I realized that I was jealous of Gemma. She was so happy in her nurse's training. But what could I do? Various friends tried to persuade me to do volunteer work, but I wanted more than that. I needed to find an identity, and I sensed that identity had something to do with paid employment.

Eventually I opened a small "natural health" center. There wasn't one in our town and I judged there was a demand. It was an enormous risk, and I had to use a lot of the money Jim had left. Everyone I talked with about it tried to dissuade me. But I had attended various training days on running small businesses, and I knew my management skills were good. I came up with a business plan that convinced the bank manager, so it opened.

It's early yet, but our heads are above water and the accountant seems pleased enough. In a sense, what I am doing is in memory of Jim. He never took time off to relax and worked under enormous stress. This center offers people the chance, through massage, aromatherapy, and hypnosis, to de-stress themselves.

Paul was furious. He told me it would be a disaster. Then when it began to be a success, he started to complain that I had changed. He told me my clothes were different, my hair was too trendy. He even accused me of trying to get another man! Nothing was further from my mind.

My relationship with Paul deteriorated to the extent that we barely talked. I also found that my friends, except for one who came into the business as a partner, didn't call anymore. "You've changed so much," one of them said. "You're confident, busy, and you've built yourself another life." I also suspected that my married friends were deliberately keeping their husbands away from me. That hurt! Surely they knew me better than that!

But I made new friends, people who didn't know me as Jim's widow. And Paul finally came around. On the day he received honors at school, he bought a huge bouquet of flowers and thanked me for showing him that hard work is one way to deal with mourning. I know it sounds like a fairy tale, but it hasn't been that easy. There are times when I long for the old days when Jim was alive. And there are nights when I feel lonely and just long to have someone there to hold me and love me.

The one thing I've learned about bereavement is the need to discover new interests, or at least to absorb onself in the old ones. To go from part of a couple to a single person in one quick blow is tough. Obviously not everyone can start their own business, but I think that somehow you've got to build some sort of life on your own. I think it's also particularly hard on women. So many of us take our identity from being Mr. Somebody's wife and then, when Mr. Somebody dies, really struggle to find out who we are.

Vivienne's story may leave us feeling inadequate, thinking, "It's all very well for her." She coped by becoming involved in business activity. Other people may need space for thought and reflection as they come to terms with their loss. But it is important to engage people's interest and participation in the human race again. To journey successfully through grief is not to emerge at the end just as before, or having forgotten what has happened. It is to emerge having lived and worked through the grief, adapting to it, and having a life that is basically enjoyable.

That life depends on circumstances, particularly on two major elements—having something to do and someone to do it *with*.

First, everyone needs something to do. If you are bereaved and are also housebound and unwell, you can enjoy listening to the radio, reading, or discovering a new interest—for example, writing poetry, doing crosswords, or sketching. Or, you could try your hand at various crafts such as needlepoint or tapestry. When you are surrounded by the same four walls day in and day out, it is essential to pursue some new interests. If you are able to get out, there is a wider range of possibilities.

This first stage—thinking of things to do—is not easy, and the best way to begin is to let yourself dream. Maybe the past few years—maybe many past years— have been centered around the needs of others. Now, you can focus on *you*. Naturally it will feel rather empty and frightening at first, but let's move on to dreaming a bit:

* Is there anything that you wanted to do in the past but didn't have time for, or that other people close to you didn't enjoy?
* Is there anything of which you've ever thought, "I'd love to try that, but..."?
* Are you open to the idea of trying to learn something new?
* What is the one thing you would most like to do in the future?
* What money could be spent on it?

Any ideas? If there were one or two that were immediately dismissed with, "But I couldn't do that at my age!" or "What would people think?" ask, "Why not?" This may be the first time in years when it's been possible to do something that you really want to do. More importantly, it may be the first time you can remember when your own needs could come first. Much of adult life is about putting other people's needs before your own, and a lifetime of doing that makes it difficult to suddenly start putting yourself first. It may even feel selfish and unchristian, but God created us with all kinds of gifts and "talents" (to use the biblical word). Perhaps this is the time to uncover some of the talents that have had to be buried in the past.

Secondly, who can share these interests? Bereaved people now living alone often feel that one of their greatest needs is for contact with other human beings. If you are in this situation, how can you go about finding that contact? How can you explore that "dream" a bit further?

Volunteer work

The range is enormous: mother and toddler groups, hospitals, seniors residences, meals on wheels, providing a break or a helping hand to caregivers, or doing something for your favorite charity. If you don't know where to start, try the city hall, the local library, the parish office, or the local social services agency. If you like working in the open air, environmental organizations and nature conservation projects frequently advertise for volunteers.

New interests, new friends

Day and evening classes offer many other possibilities. These are organized by the local public school system or university. Most classes begin at the end of September or January, or are held during the summer months. Another alternative would be taking a correspondence course, starting from the very short-term right up to a university degree.

Fitness classes, aerobics, dance, and physical activities of various sorts (not all reserved for the young and agile, but equally for the more mature) are often sponsored by the local Council for the Aging, Department of Education, and other community centers. Or there may be bowling clubs, tennis, golf, archery and fencing, swimming groups, and so on. Most state parks and national forests offer boating, fishing, and leisurely guided nature walks. In addition, the newspaper, radio, cable TV, and Internet community bulletin boards, as well as the public library, will have news and information about local events and special interest clubs. If there is no contact address given for something which catches your eye then write to the paper asking them to forward your letter. The local library will also have news of this kind.

Discussion groups offer opportunities to develop new contacts. Many institutions of higher education, womens' institutes and social groups (such as the Rotary Club, Knights of Columbus and Serra Clubs) and diocesan agencies will have an extramural adult continuing education department that organizes talks and discussions on a range of topics for members of the public. There are also groups such as the Women's Institute or the Rotary Club. Many churches run discussion groups during Advent or Lent, or RENEW/Alpha and other programs, and there's no reason at all why they can't happen at other times throughout the year. If you're concerned about going out at night, talk to your pastor or minister and see if it's possible to have one that meets during the day. If there is no general daytime activity locally for people who have time on their hands, it may be possible to start a new group—for instance, addressing the needs of newly single or bereaved people. There could be talks on coping with loneliness, cooking for one, financial advice, or home and car maintenance. Time can also be built into such meetings for people just to mingle and meet.

Socializing

One of the worst aspects of being alone is that feeling, "I can't possibly do that on my own. I'd feel awful!" If you're thinking about going to the theater or cinema, or something as simple as taking a walk, visiting a flower show, or watching a fireworks display, the secret is organization—finding out about them far enough in advance to get other people to come along. A recent census indicated that the majority of people live alone. That's an awful lot of people who might well share a sense of embarrassment about going out on their own.

If you're involved in a local church or any other community activity, why not see if you can organize a trip to the theater, a movie, or a series of local events? It only has to be a few people, and all that's needed is a date, a time, and a place to meet!

Mealtimes are another area of difficulty for people who live alone. These used to be the occasions to swap stories about what's happened during the day, or even to talk about the weather—even if they might not have been the most scintillating of conversations! But if mealtime after mealtime is now passed munching snack food while gazing at the television, it may well be time for a change.

If there are others in a similar position, why not take your courage in both hands and arrange a meal together? You don't have to be a cordon bleu chef—even a simple menu or potluck can be fun. One person could bring the first course, someone else the main course, and a third the dessert. All you do is provide the table, the cutlery, and a relaxed atmosphere in which people can feel free to chat and enjoy themselves. There's nothing mysterious or new about it. With a little courage (which you've already learned in living through bereavement), and initiative to ask a few others, many people will find they now have surprising resources!

Incidentally, in today's world of singles lifestyles, there is no need to worry about any social convention of balancing the numbers between men and women: just set up a table of all men or all women, or any combination of the two. It doesn't matter. People come together to enjoy each other's company.

A few more possibilities

Cats, dogs, and other pets make wonderful and affectionate companions and are known to reduce their owners' blood pressure! Walking a dog every day is excellent exercise, a great excuse to go out, and it's also a chance to meet other dog owners on the way. You may feel more secure walking with a dog than alone.

Do you enjoy singing or playing a musical instrument? Join a choir or music group. If you enjoy the theater, check out a local amateur drama society that welcomes new members.

New relationships

When you have lost a partner, new relationships are essential for surviving the future. Most of us need people to talk with and whose company we enjoy. But perhaps there is the prospect of a closer relationship, maybe even remarriage.

Still grieving for a husband or wife, some people remarry very quickly ("on the rebound") and then regret what they have done. Sadly, such hasty marriages can lead to a great deal of unhappiness, if not divorce. Still, there is no rule about these things, and for people who cannot bear being on their own and need a physical, loving relationship, it can work out well.

Fiona's story

No matter how soon or long after the death of a partner, a close involvement with another person does bring its own dilemmas and feelings. Fiona was widowed in her thirties, with daughters aged nine and twelve when she started working again as a teacher. Three years after her husband's death, Fiona fell in love with another teacher at the school.

At first, we just started talking over coffee or sharing a sandwich at lunchtime. We had a lot in common and enjoyed one another's company. Then one day Joseph asked if I'd like to go out for dinner that Saturday night. I felt sick! Yes, I wanted to; no, I didn't. Suddenly I felt like a teenager being asked on her first date. What if it was a disaster? What would I wear? What would I tell the girls? I said yes!

When I asked Cathy if she'd babysit her younger sister on Saturday night, they both gave me the first degree. Where was I going? Who with? Their faces dropped when I told them I was going out to dinner with a man named Joseph. Then they decided to get into it and tried to enlighten me in the ways of the world. They decided what I should wear and what color eyeshadow to put on. (In the months after that first dinner, I often remembered their enthusiasm and wondered where it had all gone.)

So Joseph and I had dinner with my daughters' blessing. It was a lovely evening and I enjoyed every minute of it. That is, until Joseph dropped me off at home. He leaned over and kissed me and said how fond of me he was becoming. I froze, pushed him away, and leaped out of the car. Upstairs in my bedroom I began to cry. I felt guilty, adulterous—as if I were being unfaithful to my dead husband—and frightened. I realized that I wasn't sure I could love anyone else and I was afraid that if I lost that person, too, I'd have to go through all the heartache again.

The next day Joseph and I talked about all of this and agreed to take things slowly. As he became more and more an important part of my life, I was feeling more distance from the girls. They said hurtful things. He was after my money; I was being disloyal to their dad; I was too old to get married again. When Joseph came over, they were rude to him or tried to ignore him. I was at my wits end and Joseph was hurt by it all. I felt I was losing my daughters. And then I discovered they had written to their grandparents on their father's side.

I thank God they did. Their grandparents came to visit and during dinner one day raised the question of Joseph and me remarrying. My daughters poured out their feelings: how they were worried that I was trying to replace their dad. I hesitatingly described how we had met and that Joseph and I loved one another. Then the children's grandfather turned to them and said, "Don't you want your mother to be happy and to know that she's loved? Because if you do, then it sounds like Joseph's the man." The girls looked disapproving. Then he said, "You know there isn't a day that passes without your grandmother and me thinking about your father. But he's dead, girls, and your mother deserves some love. If she and Joseph want to marry, then we wish them every happiness. All we ask is that you invite us to the wedding!"

And there was a wedding, six months later. Joseph and I waited to set the date until we felt the girls were ready. Gradually they let him into their lives. We all went house-hunting together and miraculously found a home that we felt we could live in. Our honeymoon became a family vacation. I'd love to say that we all lived happily ever after, but this is real life and not a fairy-tale. We've had some tough times as well as good. It's been hard for the girls to start sharing me with someone else after they'd had my undivided attention for three years. For Joseph it's been difficult discovering how to be a stepfather to two teenage girls. And me? Well, adapting to a new way of life has been stressful. Sometimes I've heard myself saying to Joseph, "But we don't do it that way in this family," and then, seeing the hurt on his face, I've had to apologize.

Through it all our relationship has grown; and the addition of Joseph to our family was nothing other than good. I think if you ask Joseph about all this, he'll just grin and say he wouldn't have life any other way.

195

In fact, that is exactly what Joseph did say, but he added, "Friends told me it would never last, and that I must be insane marrying a widow with two daughters. Well, there have been times when it helped to be crazy, but family life is always a bit crazy, isn't it?"

Putting the pieces back together again

❖ With the death of someone precious, part of us dies. A different path lies ahead. Beginning that walk, we are sometimes numb and cut off from life, sometimes clothed in loneliness and blinded by hurt and anger. But with time our steps will become lighter and more confident, and our depression will ease.

❖ There are no shortcuts on this path, and there will be difficult times. But to get this far, we have survived— even when we never thought it possible. Inside there's a streak of survival that's got us to today and that will see us through the times ahead when we feel like giving up. Other people have made it; we can too.

11

"You Feel So Helpless"
Befriending the Bereaved

I avoided my best friend after her dad died. I didn't know what to do. I said I was sorry, but Alice was so upset. I'd never seen her like that before, and I felt really embarrassed when she cried. Nobody ever tells you what you should do when a friend is grieving. I feel guilty when I think that I avoided her, but I just couldn't bear seeing her so upset.

I'm West Indian, but I've lived in Canada for nearly twenty years now. It really amazes me how much difference there is between my culture and yours when it comes to death. In my tradition, if somebody has lost a loved one, we go to the house right away. There will probably be a house full of people, and we'll be sad together. We'll talk about the person who has died, telling stories about him or her. There will be people coming and going the whole time, bringing food, offering what support they can.

The previous chapter looked at the practical steps of rebuilding a life after bereavement; this chapter gives pointers for everyone who wants to be a friend to grieving people.

Other people's experiences can be particularly valuable here, and they have been divided roughly into two areas: first, the period immediately after the bereavement; and then, later, the time for more long-term support.

The First Few Days and Weeks

Obviously a lot of what follows depends upon your relationship with the person who is grieving. Maybe it's a close friend, an acquaintance, or perhaps a neighbor or professional colleague. What is appropriate for one relationship may not be exactly the same for another. The principles are the same, however, and only require an element of sensitivity.

Marjorie's story

So often we say it's the small things that matter. Marjorie's account of how other people reacted to, and helped her through, her husband's death shows just how supportive small actions can be.

My husband died suddenly of a heart attack on his way home from work. Our two sons both work overseas, and it wasn't possible for them to spend much time with me at home. I was very much dependent on friends to see me through.

When I first heard the news of Mike's death, the police phoned my friend Isabelle and asked her to come over to stay with me. It was so good just to have someone there. She held my hand as I phoned the boys to tell them about their father's death. She came with me to the mortuary in the hospital, and moved into the spare room so I wouldn't be alone at night.

Above all, she listened. I talked, over and over again, about what Mike and I had said to each other that morning when he left for work; about how we first met and what a good husband he'd been. And every so often, some food or something to drink would appear in front of me and Isabelle would urge me to try something.

Isabelle's husband Jonathan was a great support, too. He met my sons, Andrew first and then Simon at the airport, when they flew home. He drove me to the funeral home and the hospital. I could never have driven myself—I was much too shaky! He was also good at guiding me through the practical details that come up when death happens. When I had lost both of my parents some years before, Mike had taken care of everything.

But Jonathan gently took me through the things that needed to be done now. It's not just the funeral arrangements and the registration of death. It's all the people who need to be notified. Life insurance and other insurance companies, banks, the housing authority, and IRS! There were times I felt really daunted by all the paperwork, but Jonathan guided me through it!

I also really treasured the letters and cards that arrived. Some of them were from people I didn't know—mainly people Mike had worked with through the years. But it was so heartwarming to know that they cared enough to write and tell me how sorry they'd been to hear of Mike's death. One or two of them wrote short letters with affectionate remembrances about Mike. It meant so much to read those things about my husband that I'd never known before.

Another good thing about those first few weeks were the small gifts that neighbors delivered: fruit, flowers, bottles of wine! My nearest neighbor, a dear friend, came by on the day after Mike's death and said she would do some shopping for me. I remember feeling very puzzled. Why did I need to do some shopping? She asked me what I needed, but I couldn't even think about it, so she went to look around the kitchen. Two hours later the fridge was full—which was great, because for the next few days the house was crowded. Simon and Andrew were home, distant relatives appeared, and friends dropped by.

One of the things I really valued was that Isabelle said I could phone her any time of the day or night. I knew that she meant it, too, and although I tried not to disturb her at night, there were a couple of times, about one in the morning, when I just wanted another human being to speak to. So I phoned and, true to her word, she got up and came over, letting me talk and cry until I was ready to sleep.

When I think about what I've just said, it sounds like people were really supportive. And they were, don't get me wrong. But there were some people on the street who honestly did look the other way when they saw me out walking. And I found it infuriating when other people asked me if I was feeling better now! I'd lost my husband, how on earth did they expect me to feel?

But overall, because bereavement is such an isolating experience and can really shake you up, any contact with other people becomes very important. You realize that the things we normally worry about—like the economy, and whether or not to get a new car—are nothing compared to the way we need one another.

I was so grateful when somebody would stop and talk to me if I was out in the front garden doing some weeding, or if somebody smiled at me in the supermarket. I also found I became much more sensitive to how other people might be feeling. So occasionally when I was walking in the park and saw an older person sitting alone on a bench, I'd sit down and begin a conversation. More often than not the person was also on their own after a bereavement, and we'd have a really good time sharing with one another.

So, if other people want to know how to approach the bereaved, on the basis of my experience I'd say:

1. Show that you care. A letter or card can mean so much!

2. Offer your help in practical ways. Don't ask, "Is there anything I can do?" Be specific: "Can I cut the grass/run you to the mall/accompany you somewhere?" Just remember that making decisions about everyday things is actually very difficult when you're in a state of shock, so sometimes it's a case of just thinking about what might need to be done and doing it!

3. Don't offer to help unless you really want to. There is nothing worse than accepting an offer, and then feeling that the person would really rather that you hadn't accepted.

4. Don't worry about upsetting someone who is grieving by talking about the person who has died. Nearly all of us want to talk about the loved one we've lost, and will be grateful for the opportunity to do so. If we cry, there's no need to be embarrassed—just don't try to dismiss our pain. Let us

express it. Don't worry about finding the right words to say. All we need is for you to be there and to listen.

—◆�◇◆—

Marjorie's advice has been echoed by many other bereaved people. But is there a specifically Christian input? Is there an additional element that faith can add when we are wondering how to support someone who is grieving?

Of course, there is the Christian imperative to love and care for one another, and this can be very concrete. But many people who would not call themselves Christian are just as good at caring, sometimes better.

So, is there something that is specifically Christian? There is, and it has to do with an understanding about the very nature of life itself. Christians believe that life is a gift from God, and that at death the soul returns to God. Through the life and saving death of Jesus, and as evidenced by his resurrection, they believe there is a life after death. (At this point the different Christian traditions differ in emphasis.)

But Christians also believe that the selfless example of Jesus' life was the way of God on earth. Moreover, Jesus no more wanted us flamboyantly to proclaim our religion than he did the Pharisee on the street corner outside the synagogue.

If we are going to visit someone who is newly bereaved, we need to be sensitive about what we say.

The most fervent believer will still feel pain at the loss of someone he or she loved, and it would be totally unchristian to urge the person, "Be thankful, because the person you are mourning has gone to be with the Lord." Jesus didn't say what a lucky fellow Lazarus was to be with God; he wept. The sense of loss remains, and feelings of grief are a normal, healthy human reaction.

This is not to say we must never talk of our faith, but we must be aware that sometimes it is "easier" to try to introduce optimism and cheer than it is just to feel the weight of another's pain. We must try to be conscious of who we are trying to help—the person who is grieving or ourselves. Are we trying to ease a situation because it will help the other person, or really because, deep down, we will feel more comfortable? After all, hearing another's distress is actually a harrowing experience.

These are hard thoughts to consider, but just think for a moment. How often have we asked someone how he or she is, expecting to hear, "Fine, thank you!" only to hear instead, "Well, I'm really worried that I'm going to lose my job," or words to that effect. Too often, in such a situation, we may have replied, "I'm sure you'll be fine!" and then changed the topic.

We all do it, and it is particularly true with bereavement. Getting close to another's grief can stir up all sorts of feelings in ourselves. We may be reminded of our own feelings of loss, sometimes from years ago. Or we may be reminded of our own vulnerability and mortality. That can be unnerving, and it is probably why we sometimes try to avoid such situations—it is, after all, a perfectly normal response to avoid pain. But it is not helpful for the person who is left to feel either that he or she is being ignored, or that one's grief is being denied. We need to be sensitive to what what we're doing and saying, and why we might be saying it.

But the other side of sharing someone else's pain is being able to detach ourselves from it. It is possible to get so involved that we become physically and emotionally drained. Jesus frequently needed to withdraw and spent long hours away from those to whom he ministered. We, too, need the opportunity to talk about our own reactions to someone with a sympathetic, listening ear. After sharing sadness with the bereaved person, we ourselves need time to talk with a friend or partner about how we're feeling. It needn't be a heavy session, but an opportunity to vent some bottled-up feelings.

Bill's story

Sarah and Bill lost their baby, George, when he was just four days old. They were amazed at how differently people reacted to them.

There were two doctors that we'd seen on a daily basis. The younger one seemed embarrassed by our grief. She came over and said she was sorry, and then slipped away and never came near us again. But the older one actually cried when he came to talk with us. He was obviously upset and didn't mind us knowing it. He stroked George's head, saying something like, "Sorry, George; someday we'll be able to save little guys like you, but not yet." That meant so much to us, knowing that he wasn't an unfeeling robot, and that he too was affected by George's death.

Once we were back home it was difficult to know what to tell people—for instance, people at work. As far as most of my colleagues knew, I took off for a few days of paternity leave, so I dreaded going back. In the end I asked my boss to tell one or two people, and I was sure the office gossips would soon let everyone else know.

The day I returned, the whole office went quiet for a few seconds, and then people busied themselves. Sitting on my desk was a lovely card, signed by them all, which just simply stated: "We cannot find words to say how sorry we are." A close colleague came by, and his obvious distress removed the last vestige of my protective shell. The tears started again, but not for long, and afterward I felt better and was ready to tackle some of the in-tray that had piled up in my absence.

At Christmas time, Sarah and I sent out a letter, which we had thought long and hard about sending, but finally felt it was the right thing to do. What we wanted to say to our friends and family was this:

As Christmas approaches, and people everywhere gather to celebrate the birth of the Christ child, we ask you to pray for all people like us who will be reminded of the empty crib in their own homes. It won't be an easy time for any of us.

If George had lived he would have been six months old now, and not a day passes when we don't think of him and what he might have been doing. But it wasn't to be. His heart was too badly damaged for him to live, and we firmly believe that he is now safe with his heavenly Father.

Besides asking for your prayers, we would like to thank you for all the messages of care and support you've sent over the last months. And we'd like to say: don't be afraid to talk to us about George and his death. We value the opportunity to know that he is not forgotten.

We also like to hear news of your children. So many people have begun to tell us something about a child of theirs and then said, "Oh, sorry, that was insensitive of me." But do talk to us of children and their antics. We don't want you to censor them out of your conversations with us. We're learning to live with our loss, not by avoiding it but by facing it.

We wanted to write that letter because it was obvious that some of our friends had difficulty knowing what to say to us, and we wanted to make it clear how we felt about that. Most people were really pleased that we had written it, but Sarah's mother was shocked. She thought we ought to be forgetting about George by now, and moving on to having another baby! But at least we were now able to talk about all of that with her.

When you read both Bill and Marjorie's accounts of what helped support them through bereavement and the things they themselves did, you can see how you, too, might help someone who is grieving. They are simple things really, but they are all based on letting that person know that you care. To summarize:

Don't ignore the death

Avoidance seems to be a classic reaction to bereavement, which many bereaved people have said causes them untold pain. If you can't bear facing someone, at least drop the person a note or a card.

Be practical

You can show you care by all means of practical support: mowing someone's lawn, doing the shopping, helping to clean up or running errands.

Be ready to listen

The only rule is: allow people to say what they want to say, in the way they want to say it, and be attentive. That's what listening is really about.

Remember that grief is a lengthy process

Support needs to be offered—not just in the first few days and weeks—but over months, and even years.

Support Over the Longer Period

Usually, everyone rallies in an emergency, and the same is true of a death that affects a friend, colleague, or family member. But after a few weeks the initial urgency is lost. People get caught up in their own lives again and begin to forget about the person they have been trying to help and support. For the person who was bereaved, this can herald a time of isolation. All around people are going about their everyday lives as if nothing had changed; and yet the bereaved person is living with irrevocable change—the loss of someone who was very important, who was loved. Grief is not a passing phase. It's there to be lived with and faced until adjustment is made. In the case of a major bereavement, such as the death of a spouse or child, it can take two years or more.

Timescales are never particularly helpful. It is enough to know that grieving is a long process and support should continue beyond a few weeks.

The greatest need for long-term support from others is, of course, after the loss of a partner. The widow or widower has not only lost a husband or wife, but the life that they lived together and the support that they gave to one another. Beginning to face the future means learning to live without the support that marriage gave and, in many cases, learning to live alone.

Earlier in this chapter, Marjorie described the support she received in the early days after her husband's death. Three years after his death did she still need support?

I don't like to think of it as support. But, do I need the time and friendship of other people? Oh, yes, most definitely. I've gotten used to living on my own, but if I had to go more than a couple of days without having a good conversation with someone, I'd go crazy!

The loneliness is the worst thing of all. We were married for thirty-three years when Mike died, and during that time I think I spent only a handful of nights without him. Even though some nights we'd just sit in front of the television and not talk much, at least he was there! Now there are a lot of evenings when I come back late in the afternoon and know that I'm on my own till the morning. It makes the evenings seem really long. There are nights I look at my watch and can't believe it's only nine o'clock. It feels like it ought to be midnight!

That's why I love invitations to go out at night—not for anything special, but just to spend the evening with others. Isabelle and Jonathan have me over about once a week, and we have some supper and play Scrabble. I'm always worried about being a burden to them, but they keep saying I'm not. I'd hate it if they ever thought, "Oh, no, we have to have Marjorie over again this week." That would be awful.

I go to our parish church every Sunday, but they don't have much going on during the week—not at night, anyway. It's fine if you're a Brownie or a Boy Scout, but I'm a little old for that! Sometimes I think the church forgets there are lots of people on their own.

I've recently become good friends with two other widows whom I met through our bereavement support group. Now and then we'll go to the cinema or theater, and we often meet for coffee. Sometimes I just long to be part of a family again. Once a year each of my sons comes home with his wife and children and, apart from the fact that I love seeing them, you have no idea how different it feels to go out. I feel like I actually "belong" to someone. I suppose that it sounds odd, but when we go for a walk along the river and pass other people, I can look them in the eye and smile and say hello. Usually they smile back. But when I'm alone and pass someone, sometimes I just don't feel safe. And other times when I do greet them, they look startled and turn away.

Another thing I'd say to people who have widowed friends is that sometimes you need to exert a bit of gentle pressure. I've always been a cheerful person and enjoyed getting out, but about a year or so after Mike's death I just couldn't be bothered to do anything. It was too much effort to dress up, and I'd be scared of meeting new people or being in new situations.

Looking back, I suppose I was suffering from a mild depression, but Isabelle kept persevering. She'd phone up and ask me to do something like come over for a meal on Saturday night. And when I'd hesitate or think of some excuse, she'd find a way around it. She'd come and pick me up. Then when I got there I would enjoy myself, but it took some effort to get me there!

I can see how easy it is to slip into the habit of saying "no" to things. Then people give up on you, and never ask you to anything. Fortunately, Isabelle wasn't good at taking "no" for an answer. But she didn't pressure me, either. I think she could sense that there were times when I should be on my own, and times when a little company was all I needed.

Drawing from Marjorie's experience, and others in similar situations, there seem to be several ways to be a good friend over a longer period.

Share your time

It's always hard adapting to change, whatever the reason. Major bereavement creates a void that only a long period of adjustment can fill. During and after that time, it's good to have friends who won't demand dazzling company, but who will let the grieving person talk about what he or she is feeling without getting embarrassed or trying to change the subject. So if you can offer time, a warm welcome, a listening ear, or even just another brain on a crossword puzzle, then you will be of help.

It's good, too, if you knew the person who died. Don't be afraid to talk about the past, because sharing memories is often welcomed by the grieving.

Coax, but don't pressure

There's only a thin dividing line between these two. Nothing is worse than forcing another person to do something he or she just doesn't want to do. Equally, many bereaved people may need a little coaxing if you're thinking of including them in an outing or a meal. The difficulty is knowing when to accept "no" for an answer. Just try to be sensitive.

Urge patience

After the first few weeks, some bereaved people talk of making major life changes—selling the family home, or moving away to a completely new part of the country. These are such life-changing decisions that they need to be made with much thought, and not in the emotional turmoil of a recent bereavement.

If you can, urge patience and recommend that the decision be postponed until a certain period of time has elapsed, such as six months or a year.

Be alert

There may be some practical ways to help. Immediately after the death you may have suggested things you could do to help, but stopped because time has moved on. Yet there may still be things that you can do.

Offer your hand with some decorating, car maintenance, or even some gardening. It may well be that another pair of hands helps complete a chore that would otherwise have been left undone.

Making tedious telephone calls can be a particular ordeal for those who have been bereaved—for instance, to find an estimate for some house maintenance or to rectify the gas or electricity services. Perhaps you might call for the person. Having such jobs completed can really boost one's morale.

Writing Christmas cards is another very difficult task for those who have lost a partner or a child. You can't write someone's cards for them, but simply being present may be a comfort, and you could offer to address envelopes or help in some other way.

Don't slink away

In supporting a friend through bereavement, try to be honest. If you find that you are not happy with the demands being made on you, try to say so—not nastily, or angrily, but with sensitivity. It might feel more comfortable to put the answering machine on for the next few weeks and be unavailable, but the bereaved person will be left in the dark, wondering if he or she has caused some offense.

It's fairer to say to the person, "I'm so sorry, but I'm afraid it's getting a bit difficult when you phone every night at midnight. It would be fine about nine, but if nights are hard, perhaps you would let me help you find some other people to talk to?"

If you do find yourself looking for excuses to avoid your friend's company, ask yourself why. Is it because you find your friend's conversation depressing, even boring? Perhaps there's a little voice saying, "I wish she'd cheer up, she ought to be getting over it by now!" Maybe it's because you need a bit of light relief. After all, a day by day reminder of mortality can be tough on anyone.

Nobody would condemn you for feeling like this. It's perfectly understandable. See if you can find an outlet elsewhere: other friends, a swim, a good book, even a favorite television program. Then you will have more energy to listen with compassion. Above all, don't feel guilty. Don't confuse your very real need for a break with a reaction against your friend. You may have to continue supporting and befriending that person for a long time. You cannot do this with resentment in your heart, or try to "extricate" yourself by becoming inexplicably busy or unavailable.

The need for professional help

Occasionally the normal process of bereavement can "get stuck," or depressive illness can occur. The difficulty is knowing when professional help is required. General practitioners sometimes have difficulty in recognizing serious depression, so how can you tell the warning signs?

While you cannot be expected to diagnose when a friend's grief might need more help than you and others can give, on the other hand, if you are not alert to it, who else will be?

If you are becoming concerned, you might try contacting one of the organizations listed at the back of this book for groups or "consultation" services in your area. They have professional experience, and your friend can benefit from contacting them. Sometimes the opportunity to talk with other people who have gone through a similar experience can be extremely uplifting. Then again, you may notice symptoms of depression—difficulty in sleeping, early wakening, loss of appetite, poor concentration, talk of suicide. Try to encourage the person to seek professional help. If necessary, accompany your friend. Your observations can help underline the seriousness of symptoms.

Visiting a counselor who specializes in bereavement or seeking psychiatric help can be extremely beneficial. Obviously not everyone needs such help, but at times it is necessary. If it is felt to be necessary by the primary care physician, be supportive. Despite the mistaken stigma attached to seeking such help, it should be no different from consulting any other specialist. Whatever you do, don't back off now. Your support and friendship are even more critical.

You feel so helpless

❖ Supporting the bereaved is no mystery and requires no special skills. The key contribution you have to make is your friendship, your time, and your common sense. Use your eyes and ears to see what might be needed in practical terms, and make yourself available.

❖ Initially, don't wait to be asked to help or worry about intruding. Equally, don't ask questions that require some kind of decision. Grief begins with a state of shock, and it is very difficult to think logically or to make decisions.

❖ For the longer term, remember that grieving lasts a long time and can leave problems of loneliness or a sense of uselessness. Just be there as a true friend—to listen, to encourage, and to let someone know he or she hasn't been forgotten. The Bible calls it "loving kindness."

12

Struggling to Make Sense of It All
Death as Part of Life

I was devastated when my son Gordon died four years ago. He was just sixteen. Even now I can see no purpose in it whatsoever. If I have learned anything at all from the depression and agony, it is that love is very precious.

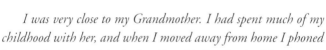

I was very close to my Grandmother. I had spent much of my childhood with her, and when I moved away from home I phoned her regularly and visited when I could. But her health started to fail, and she was forced to move into assisted living. Only two months later, she died. Obviously I was sad she had gone, but I could see it was right. She'd said she was ready to die, and she was!

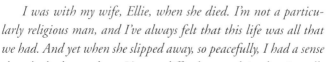

I was with my wife, Ellie, when she died. I'm not a particularly religious man, and I've always felt that this life was all that we had. And yet when she slipped away, so peacefully, I had a sense that she had moved on. It's very difficult to explain, but it really made me think that there is another world beyond this one.

The reason that the title of this chapter is "Struggling to Make Sense of It All" is because that is all we can ever attempt to do. There are things that we have hunches about. We might say we have faith. If we're really keen-intense, perhaps we might have even read theological textbooks! But none of this gives us any ultimate proof. Even books can fall short. How do we begin to find answers that satisfy us when we ask why we are born, why we die, and whether there is a life after death?

Some people find wisdom within one of the different branches of Christianity or other world religions. Others turn to philosophy. Spiritualists would say that they have proof of the human spirit's survival beyond death (although there is something strange about trying to make sense of life and death by a process which is fixed on a "world" which only the spiritualist can see), and in recent years there has been a great deal of interest in "near-death experiences." Or perhaps we shouldn't be asking questions at all, as long as we have faith.

Maria's story

Maria asked questions and did find partial answers through the suffering and death of her husband, Tom. She is a lively, dynamic woman in her forties, and Tom died at home from a particularly virulent cancer. Their three teenage children were all at home during this time.

Tom had just turned thirty-eight when it was discovered that a mole on his back was a malignant melanoma. Both of us were shocked. We didn't tell the children about it; we believed the doctors who assured us that it had been caught quickly enough.

We thanked God that we'd been encouraged to seek medical help so quickly, and we joked about it as "an intimation of mortality"—a timely reminder that none of us is here forever. But what we didn't joke about was how much it had reminded us that we loved and needed each other. Those first few weeks after we had heard that Tom should be "in the clear" were like a second honeymoon. Our loving and being loved was better than ever, because we knew each other so well and had shared so much throughout our marriage.

We promised we would never again take each other for granted, and started going to church again. When the children were younger we used to go every week as a family, but gradually the habit had slipped; somehow God had been squeezed out of our busy schedule. But Tom's brush with cancer jolted us, and together we decided that it was time to bring the spiritual sharing back into our life together. The children were very skeptical when Tom and I announced that we were going to church and that they were welcome to come with us. There was a unanimous cry of, "No way!" Then Sarah, the youngest, asked us why we were starting to go again. It was time to be clear with them.

It took a while to reassure them that their dad was going to be okay, but eventually they said they believed us. Sarah decided she'd come to church too, so that she could ask God to make sure that her dad was going to be all right. Sarah was ten at the time. The other two— Lori was thirteen and George was fifteen—considered themselves atheists and scoffed at her, but Sarah, true to her word, joined us.

I enjoyed going back to church, and found a joy and comfort there. It was like returning to a familiar place, and after, I felt that this was where I was meant to be— that seemed strange! Tom, too, had been really glad that we had gone, and said ironically that he was glad the melanoma had been discovered. "It's reminded me of the real priorities in life," he said.

The next few months were idyllic. It was so good to be alive. Everything seemed to come together, and Tom and I allowed ourselves to reach out to God again, enjoying our rediscovered faith.

Then Tom became ill. He lost his energy and appetite, and started to experience abdominal pain. We prayed that it was something like appendicitis, but deep down we feared the worst.

We were right. The malignant melanoma had not been caught as early as the doctors had thought. Tom's cancer had spread.

We were devastated. Tom began rigorous medical treatments, and we found ourselves asking, "Why?" Surely the initial diagnosis had been the jolt that God had "wanted," to bring us back to him. What more could be gained from this torment?

One night I went through what I can only call "the long, dark night of the soul." Tom was back in the hospital, the children were asleep, and the house was quiet. I couldn't settle down. Inside a voice kept saying, "A God of love wouldn't do this to you!" And I couldn't answer. Yet I needed to know that God was for real and really loves us. I considered the evidence against this:

pain, suffering, war, starvation, poverty, loneliness. The world appeared to be a very bleak place indeed. But then I realized that so many of these nightmare situations were man-made. God hadn't caused them.

But the nagging voice persisted, "If Tom dies, after all your prayers for him to live, isn't that a sign there is no God?" And for a time the "voice" won. I was desolate at the thought of having to live without Tom. I felt cold and lonely and deeply afraid. No, it wasn't possible, it was too much to bear. I began to cry—with self-pity, with fear, with hopelessness. "God, if you're really there, if you are really with us in all of this, show me!" I prayed it over and over again, but I found no answer.

Every hour the clock chimed, proclaiming the relentless march of time. Still I had no answer. I tried to read my Bible, but couldn't. I remembered life before Tom; the day we met; our wedding day; the children's births. What had it all been for?

And then, just before dawn, the birdsongs began. Noisily a chorus announced the dawn of a new day. I pulled the curtains back, and watched as the dark sky slowly began to lighten. I could not see the sun, but it was starting to emerge. Again night had turned to day. And it was only then that my panic began to recede. I felt a part of a continuum of time. Since the world began, millions of years ago, every day had begun this way. Generation after generation had been born, lived, and then died. And Tom and I and the children were a part of a living generation for only a relatively short time. Our death, I realized, is a part of God's plan for the world. Just as the sun keeps rising, we need to die, ready to experience whatever lies beyond death.

My answer had begun! Intuitively I knew that Tom was going to die soon. But I found comfort in accepting that death is part of life. I don't believe that God makes bad things happen to us. Tom's cancer probably had more to do with human destruction of the planet through damaging the ozone layer than with God's deliberate intention to strike Tom down. I was prepared to trust God in whatever lay ahead.

Some of our new friends from church told us that all we had to do was pray harder, or visit a Christian healer, or repent and Tom would be healed. God, they said, was waiting to show us his power in a remarkable way. Now, years later, I realize that it was convenient for them to say such things, and then blame Tom and me when things got worse. Instead, it would be difficult to hear our pain and confusion about what was happening to Tom.

Two people helped us at that time: Liz, our deacon's wife, and the hospital chaplain. Liz struggles daily with chronic pain from arthritis and, in the hours that she spent with Tom and me, I sensed that her own pain made it possible to share in ours. When we asked the question "Why?", she never rushed in to answer. She just talked of the incomplete answers she had discovered to her own question of "Why?"

The chaplain helped me to understand and accept that incomplete answers are probably all that I could expect in my lifetime. Life would be different if we knew exactly what happened after death, or how to manipulate God just by praying hard enough. Where would the mystery be then, and what would be the point of faith?

As I had known intuitively, Tom's treatment did not work. Nothing more could be done for him than to relieve his pain. Tom came home to die.

The chaplain urged us to pray for the fruits of the Spirit: love, joy, peace, patience, kindness, goodness, faithfulness, self-control, and gentleness. He also urged us to be honest with God about all that we felt—to cast into God's hands all of our confusion and hurt and anger. All those things were still there, despite my acceptance of death as a part of life and as a part of God's plan for us. We love, and, therefore, we are bound to feel pain when we are separated by death.

Our daily prayer was that, as a family living with the knowledge that we were soon to lose Tom, the Holy Spirit would work within us. We told God that we did not understand why this was happening to us, but asked for help to take our confusion and pain and to help us in our despair.

When I look back I can see that we had moved beyond words, and that all of our lives were part of that prayer. When I washed Tom—he was too weak to wash himself—I felt a giving from my heart. It became an act of such tenderness and love that I just know God was ministering to Tom through me. I know it sounds strange, but touching Tom felt sacramental—an outward and visible sign of an inner, life-giving grace. It was as if Tom was being bathed not just with soap and water, but with the very love of God.

We all became very close as a family. Our two "resident atheists," who at first exhibited enormous anger—and quite rightly so—at their father's terminal illness, mellowed and had long conversations with their father about the meaning of life. They became more thoughtful, caring people who value life. Being so close to their father during his last weeks, and being present when he died, touched them deeply. Together we witnessed Tom's transformation and peacefulness as he approached death.

My own perception of life shifted with Tom's death. Everything I had accepted intellectually, I now knew as real. I could see, three days before Tom died, that his body could take very little more. It had become so helpless and emaciated that I could only pray it wouldn't be much longer. Mercifully, effective drug treatments meant that Tom wasn't in pain, though he slept a lot. When he woke, Tom, the true Tom, was strong and glad that he would soon be free.

Tom was ready to die, and we were ready for him to go. We all said goodbye in our different ways, and not one of us could wish for him to live longer than necessary in that poor, ravaged body. So the night he died, we were all there at the bedside, talking to him, holding him. He was in a coma by this time, and his breathing had become very labored. As the four of us sat there, keeping our vigil of love, I pondered the parallel to our children's birth.

Then I had been the one who labored, while Tom encouraged—as my body struggled to bring new life into the world. Now that same new life, about to grow into adulthood, watched and waited as their father was born into the next world. We were there supporting him as he journeyed on to the next life.

That realization was one of those moments when heaven and earth become one. Captured in that moment was the meaning of life itself, and I finally understood how transitory this world really is and sensed the presence of eternity. At the moment of Tom's death there was such a sense of God and the whole communion of saints with us, offering comfort and welcoming Tom, that I cried with ecstasy.

I rarely talk about this because it's very difficult to find the words to describe such an overwhelming feeling. Through Tom's death I have learned so much about life and our place within God's purpose. I'm not afraid of death anymore, and although I miss Tom enormously, I'm convinced that one day we'll be reunited.

Knowing what I know now, would I go through it again? Of course not! I'm only human; and if I could wave a magic wand, my wish would be that Tom hadn't become ill and died, and that we were still together as a family. But life just isn't like that. It moves on relentlessly. Were Tom still alive we'd still have to cope with the children finding their independence and leaving home. Nothing remains the same forever.

And that, for me, is the meaning of life. We might think we've built a safe cocoon—and that cocoon can be wealth, achievement, health, even faith—but it isn't sacrosanct. When our defenses are down, we are all vulnerable people who need one another and who need to feel loved. At the heart of that love is God.

Maria's moving account illustrates how death itself can be seen positively. This is not to say that there will be no grief and no sense of loss. Such feelings are inevitable and healthy. With the words of the apostle Paul in the first letter to the Corinthians, it is possible to say:

For this perishable body must put on imperishability, and this mortal body must put on immortality. When this perishable body puts on imperishability, and this mortal body puts on immortality, then the saying that is written will be fulfilled:

"Death has been swallowed up in victory."
"Where, O death, is your victory?
Where, O death, is your sting?" (1 Cor 15:53-55)

But do we move on? Does the mortal put on the immortal? Even without faith it is difficult to believe that this life is all that we have. The universe, the planets, the sheer complexity and variety of plant, animal, and human life, make it harder to believe that it all came into being through some accident than to accept that God, the divine designer, called it into being.

With faith, we can celebrate the real purpose to our lives. From the very first stirring of life, when we were being nurtured in our mother's womb, a pattern for our lives was laid. The pattern determined whether our hair would be blond or black, whether we were geniuses or gentle plodders, and it put into place our very own unique, genetic make-up. One more divine original!

None of this proves an existence after death. It does point to the complexity of life and offers reasonable evidence for what we may not understand. Can anyone prove there is nothing beyond this life?

Christians believe that Jesus lived, died, and rose again. Thinkers and theologians have disputed its full meaning. We need to turn to the New Testament, to the accounts of Christ's resurrection, to seek to understand those accounts.

There is no doubt that Jesus' followers believed something momentous had happened. Why would a group of dejected, defeated disciples, whose teacher had just been put to death in a most public and humiliating way, be transformed into a movement of energy and vitality? The defeated followers claimed that Jesus had risen from the dead. Despite accusations of mass hysteria or hallucination, the Gospels recount several resurrection appearances to different people at different times: to Mary Magdalene at the tomb; to the disciples gathered together and hiding; to Thomas eight days later; again, when the disciples were together; to Simon Peter and some of the other disciples when they were fishing at the Sea of Tiberias; and to the two disciples walking on the road to Emmaus. In this last account two men are joined by a stranger. They describe what has happened to Jesus, including reports that his body is missing from the tomb. The stranger stays with them and later, when he breaks bread with them, they realize that they, too, have seen the risen Christ. Full of excitement, they race back to Jerusalem.

For many people these accounts are convincing evidence that Jesus survived beyond death. They do not tell us what that survival is like, what happens in heaven, or what it all means. But they do tell us that life is more than death.

Could it all be wishful thinking? None of us likes to think that we will cease to exist. Throughout history, society after society has spoken and planned for an afterlife. Egyptian pharaohs were buried with the things they would require. The spirits of ancestors have been revered in many tribal cultures, and religions throughout the world have tried to make sense of death. Deep within each one of us there is an instinct that life persists in some form beyond death. It might be wishful thinking, or it might be a perception of truth. Fear of death versus purpose in death? It's the paradox in which we are forced to live.

If, however, what happens beyond death really is still confined to the world of faith or the mystical, can we draw any insight from life this side of the grave?

Birth into this world offers us a life experience in which to learn to grow and to develop in body, mind, and spirit. We form relationships and we learn to love. We are inspired by acts of immense heroism and self-sacrifice, and we are appalled by examples of inhumanity. We may be moved to creativity or bored by tedium. We may father and mother new life. We may nurture life in other ways. But just as nature lives through the four seasons, from spring to summer, from autumn to winter, human beings are also part of the cycle of life and death. No wonder the words of the book of Ecclesiastes find resonance with so many people:

For everything there is a season, and a time for every matter under heaven:

a time to be born, and a time to die;

a time to plant, and a time to pluck up what is planted;

a time to kill, and a time to heal... (3:1-3).

The problem with this passage comes when people die before the "right" season, that is, long before their three-score and ten years. As so many of the accounts in this book have shown, death brings grief and sorrow in its wake, and some deaths just seem tragic and outrageous. There is too much overwhelming loss to write happily of victory through death. It would be arrogant and unfeeling. And it is impossible to see any purpose in needless famine, or any victory in the deaths of thousands of innocent people through war.

There is a lot of physical, emotional, and mental pain in life. The New Testament of Jesus, however, is not just about the resurrection, but also about Jesus who was born as the Son of man. In Jesus' life on earth we see God caring deeply about the things that make human beings hurt—sickness, being a social outcast, being lost. In his life, his ministry, and his death, Jesus shows us a God who is with us in our pain, and who knows our being at its very worst.

The message of Jesus is a simple one: heal the sick, accept the outcast, and find the lost. In other words, love one another, just as your Father in heaven loves you. On this precept is built the Kingdom of God.

Time after time, though, that message is ignored, and some of the most tragic sequences in human history have resulted—not from a vengeful God determined to punish his erring people, but from our own willfulness and selfishness. In a fallen world marred by inhumanity and injustice, even when it is transformed through love and compassion, how is it possible to claim that death has not won?

Sadly, for some people the question remains unanswerable. For others, their experience and their faith (as in Maria's account earlier) tell them that this life is the channel for the next. Not an easy exit, but a labor of love that delivers to God our soul and our spirit, shaped and refined by our dealings with others and molded by life's experience, no matter how short or long.

Understanding our lives as the place where we grow spiritually before entering the Kingdom of heaven may not seem to sufficiently explain the deaths of babies, young children, and those who had little opportunity to develop. Yet our own timescales and human perspectives are not those of God. We do not know, and in this lifetime can never know, the exact purposes of God and the whole of his creation.

In our day-to-day living, and in our relationships with those we love and who love us, we can value the life that we do have. We cannot hold on to it forever. In the Sermon on the Mount, Jesus warns us not to worry about tomorrow; each day has troubles enough of its own. "Live each day as if it were your last" may seem a tall order, but it has a legitimate heritage!

Marion's story

Marion's mother, Beth, was widowed during the Second World War. At that time Marion was just three years old; and as long as she could remember, her only parent had been her mother. There were no brothers or sisters, and when she thought back, Marion could see how close she and her mother were.

It was only when Marion married a man she had met at the factory where she worked that she moved away from the home she'd lived in all those years.

I knew Mom was heartbroken that I had gone, although she was glad that I was finally getting married. (Not that I went far, because Bill and I moved into an apartment just a few streets away from her.) I used to worry about her and how she was going to cope. But she seemed to adapt quite well. She always came to be with us for Sunday lunch, or we'd go to her house, and I stopped over when I could.

Although she was well into her sixties by this stage, the next thing I knew she became a volunteer housekeeper/nurse's aid for social services. When I asked her whether this was a wise thing to do, I'll never forget what she said: "Marion, all my life I've had someone to care for. First it was my own mother, and then your dad, God rest their souls, and then it was you. But you've got your own home now, and after a lifetime of having someone to look after, I can't stop now."

Bill and I soon had our first baby, a little daughter, and life continued much as before—apart from the interrupted nights. Mom loved Sara and spoiled her rotten. It really made her day if I asked her to take Sara for a couple of hours while I went shopping.

About this time home-bound services ceased for cost reasons. Though Mom was a little put out to begin with, she'd found an elderly neighbor or two for whom she could do errands, and seemed quite happy.

It must have been the year Mom turned seventy-four that I suddenly realized she had aged. Until then I could have sworn that she had looked the same for ages, but that year she began to look frail. She walked awkwardly, forgot things, and she began to get moody in a way I'd never seen before. Even Sara, who adored her grandma, said that she was no fun anymore.

I worried a lot about it, but Bill wasn't very sympathetic. In the end, I talked to the family doctor and he said he'd drop in on Mom. He phoned the next day and asked me to come in to talk with him. Basically his message was that he was shocked by Mom's deterioration and concerned that she wasn't able to look after herself anymore. Had I thought about her coming to live with me?

When I spoke with Mom, I might as well have suggested that she go to live on the moon. She was livid. That doctor had no right to poke his nose into her business, I think was how she described it. So I left her in her own home, visiting at least twice a day. But then one day she didn't answer the door. She was still in bed, ashen white, and only barely conscious.

At the hospital I was advised to either take her into my own home or find assisted living for her. The blood supply to her brain was malfunctioning, and she kept passing out. There was nothing they could do for her. And so, after a few days, Mom came home with me. She cried, she sulked, and she refused to come out of her room. She just wasn't herself anymore. It wasn't long before this hostile stranger was causing fights between Bill and me. Bill begged me to find a home for her, but I couldn't. All my life Mom had been there for me, and now I wanted to be there for her.

It was all so incredibly sad. This lovely person deep down, who cared for so many people in her lifetime, now needed the care of others, but she hated it. She couldn't adapt to a quiet life. Rather than knit, or read, or watch television, she just seemed to get angry because she couldn't do what she wanted.

Eventually I couldn't bear it any longer and confronted her. This time, instead of telling me to go away, she cried. Out it all came, and I realized how difficult it is for independent people to admit their own needs. She hated not having the strength to do things that she used to do, and admitted that she was afraid that the next time she passed out she would never wake up again.

I don't think there's anything in life that prepares you for the time when you see a parent become fragile and almost childlike. And then when they reveal their own deep-seated fears, and they are no longer strong and protective of you, it is absolutely discouraging.

So Mom and I sat there on her bed, both crying. Silently I prayed that I would find the words to comfort her. I was completely at a loss, with no idea what to say. So I just told her how much I loved her and how much she'd given me over the years, and that now I'd like to return some of that love by caring for her.

We got very close again after that. She became much easier to be with, and I tried to be sensitive: protecting her privacy and arranging activities for her to do. She enjoyed helping with the cooking, and quite often I'd hear her and Sara in the kitchen together, chatting about all sorts of things.

It was only a few days later though that Mom had a nasty fall. She'd obviously passed out again, and this time she broke her arm. They kept her in the hospital, so Sara and I headed there for visiting hours.

Mom was quite distracted and her thoughts seemed miles away. She turned to me and said, "Marion, you know I was so afraid of dying. Well, I just want to say that I'm not anymore. I've had lots of dreams about it recently, and I've dreamt about my own Mamma and Pa, and about your Dad, and I kind of sense that they're waiting for me to join them."

I was really taken aback. Mom was one of those solid, down-to-earth types and I had never heard her talking about dreams before. It's the kind of thing she'd usually dismiss as nonsense. So I just nodded and waited to see what was going to happen next.

"I think I'm ready to die now. I'm tired of being such a burden. My bones are old, and it's time they had a rest. You've been really good to me, looking after me, but it's not the same as being in my own home. I think there's another home waiting for me now, and I'm just waiting for the angels to take me there."

That was quite a speech for Mom. But she was relaxed now, and seemed very peaceful. We talked a bit about things that we'd done in the past, and Sara listened as her grandma talked about how she felt after my dad died. Then it was the end of visiting time. When I said goodbye, I just knew it was the last time I'd see Mom alive. Don't ask me how, but I did. Our eyes met, and it was then I knew she felt the same way. We didn't say anything, just kept looking, and then she smiled and patted my hand.

After we left I found myself walking toward the chapel. Sara said she would wait for me outside, and so I was alone when a nun who served in hospital ministry came up and asked if I'd like to talk. I said no, but asked if she'd say a prayer for my mom. I just couldn't find the words. So she did, and as she prayed I cried. I had this picture in my mind of me handing over Mom to Jesus, and asking him to love her like I did. And then I realized that he already did, and that it was right for Mom to die now. She was ready.

Early next morning the phone rang. The hospital was calling to say that Mom had died in her sleep. I wasn't surprised, and although I was still really upset, I knew that Mom would be happy. Later on I talked to Sister Maria, the nun at the hospital, about it, and she said that though I was glad for Mom's sake, it didn't mean that I couldn't mourn her.

That was good advice, because I missed Mom like crazy. I kept going into her room expecting her to be there, and then I cleared out her old house and felt that there was so much of her I never knew. Yet every time I took flowers to her grave, I felt at peace with the world and one with God. There really is a time to be born, and a time to die.

It's impossible to summarize a chapter about struggling to make sense of it all. In not finding all the answers, and in struggling together through faith and love, the paradox is that we can come closer to God. Suffering is not the opposite of love, but rather an integral and productive part of it. It's not that we should seek pain in our lives in order to grow—that would be macabre and masochistic. But living through pain is extremely important, even the bitter pain of the death of a partner. And in the aching pain and confusion and emptiness of our bereavement; and in the kindness and comfort of others, we find God, the very author of love itself.

So let us value life—all of it. Life is a gift from God. As we laugh and cry, love and argue, let us live it as fully as we can. We can't hoard it; we can't lock it in a safety deposit box. We never know when it may end. And on the days when the pain of loving caused by death seems too much to bear, we can draw courage from the knowledge that God shares it all with us. He mourns with us, he strengthens us, and he helps us to prepare for the day when we, too, will enter into the glory of the kingdom that lies beyond this world. Then, we will fully understand why we are born, and live, and die.

Organizations That Offer Information and Other Resources

There are many organizations, church groups, and individual counselors who offer a listening ear to bereaved people who would like to talk about what they are going through, or who are looking for advice. Many of these are local initiatives and you will find out about them by asking around: the GP medical practice, the library, the church, social services, or a local hospice. This list features national organizations that offer helplines, support groups, or information (printed and online).

National Catholic Ministry to the Bereaved
26700 Euclid Avenue
Cleveland OH 44092-2527
440-943-3480
www.griefwork.org

Bereaved Families of Ontario
36 Eglinton Avenue West, Suite 602
Toronto, ON CANADA M4R 1A1
416-440-0290
www.bereavedfamilies.net
Bereaved helping the bereaved learn to live with grief.

The Compassionate Friends
P.O. Box 3696
Oak Brook, IL 60522-3696
630-990-0010   877-969-0010
www.compassionatefriends.org
Grief support after the death of a child. The secret of TCF's success is simple: as seasoned grievers reach out to the newly

bereaved, energy that has been directed inward begins to flow outward and both are helped to heal.

The Compassionate Friends Canadian National Office
P.O. Box 141 R.P.O. Corydon
Winnipeg, MB CANADA R3M 3S7
204-475-6693   866-823-0141
secretary@tcfcanada.net www.thecompassionatefriend.org
An international/non-profit, non-denominational/self-help organization, offering friendship, understanding, grief education, and HOPE for the future to all families who have experienced the death of a child of any age, from any cause.

SHARE Pregnancy & Infant Loss Support, Inc.
National Office
St. Joseph Health Center
300 First Capitol Drive
St. Charles, MO 63301-2893
636-947-6164
800-821-6819
www.nationalshareoffice.com
A not-for-profit nondenominational organization providing support for those whose lives are touched by the tragic death of a baby through early pregnancy loss, stillbirth, or newborn death.

Sudden, Infant Death Syndrome (SIDS) Alliance
1314 Bedford Avenue, Suite 210
Baltimore, MD 21208
410-653-8226
800-221-7437
www.sidsalliance.org
Support for families experiencing the death of a baby or anyone seeking the latest, quality-assured information about SIDS and ways to reduce the risk of infant death.

Alive Alone
11115 Dull Robinson Road
Van Wert, OH 45891
419-238-7879
www.alivealone.org
An organization for education and charitable purposes to benefit bereaved parents whose only child or all children are deceased, by providing a self-help network and publications to promote communication and healing, to assist in resolving their grief, and a means to reinvest their lives for a positive future.

National Association for Widowed People
P.O. Box 3564
Springfield IL 62708
503-775-5683

SAVE-Suicide Awareness Voices of Education
7317 Cahill Road, Suite 207
Minneapolis, MN 55439-2080
952-946-7998   888-511-SAVE   1-800-784-2433 (hotline)
www.save.org
Suicide Awareness Voices of Education (SAVE) is an organization dedicated to educating the public about suicide prevention and to speak for suicide survivors.

American Association of Suicidology
4201 Connecticut Avenue, NW, Suite 408
Washington, D.C. 20008
202-237-2280
www.suicidology.org
Dedicated to understanding and prevention of suicide.

The National Hospice and Palliative Care Organization
1700 Diagonal Road, Suite 300
Alexandria, VA 22314
800-658-8898 (Help line)
www.nhpco.org
Valuing the experience of the end of life. A team-oriented approach for expert medical care, pain management, emotional and spiritual support expressly tailored to the patient's wishes and to the family and loved ones. English and Spanish language website.

The Gift Foundation
P.O. Box 95
Carpentersville, IL 60110
800-421-GIFT
www.giftfoundation.org

Other Books That You May Find Helpful

Ashley, Benedict M., OP and Kevin D. O'Rourke, OP. *Health Care Ethics: A Theological Analysis, Fourth Edition.* Washington, D.C.: Georgetown University Press, 1997.

Bernardin, Joseph L. Cardinal. *The Gift of Peace: Personal Reflections.* Chicago: Loyola Press, 1997.

Bosco, Antoinette. *Shaken Faith: Hanging in There When God Seems Far Away.* Mystic, CT: Twenty-Third Publications, 2001.

Kübler-Ross, Elizabeth. *On Death and Dying.* New York: Macmillan Publishing Company, 1969.

Lewis, C. S. *A Grief Observed.* New York: Bantam, Doubleday, Dell, Inc., 1976.

Martin, Sheila. *Saying Goodbye with Love: A Step-by-Step Guide Through the Details of Death.* New York: Crossroad Publishing Company, 1999.

National Conference of Catholic Bishops, Committee on the Liturgy. *Reflections on the Body, Cremation and Catholic Funeral Rites.* Washington, D.C., 1997.

Nelson, Jan and David Aaker. *Bereavement Ministry.* Notre Dame, IN: Ave Maria Press, 1998. Includes lists of support resources according to topic, e.g., for those grieving a miscarriage or stillbirth, suicide, etc.

Nouwen, Henri J. *Our Greatest Gift.* San Francisco: Harper San Francisco, 1995.

O'Keefe Lafser, Christine. *Longing for My Child.* Chicago: Loyola Press, 2002.

Rupp, Joyce. *Praying Our Goodbyes.* New York: Random House, 1992.

BOOKS & MEDIA

The Daughters of St. Paul operate book and media centers at the following addresses. Visit, call or write the one nearest you today, or find us on the World Wide Web, www.pauline.org

CALIFORNIA

3908 Sepulveda Blvd, Culver City, CA 90230	310-397-8676
5945 Balboa Avenue, San Diego, CA 92111	858-565-9181
46 Geary Street, San Francisco, CA 94108	415-781-5180

FLORIDA

145 S.W. 107th Avenue, Miami, FL 33174	305-559-6715

HAWAII

1143 Bishop Street, Honolulu, HI 96813	808-521-2731
Neighbor Islands call:	866-521-2731

ILLINOIS

172 North Michigan Avenue, Chicago, IL 60601	312-346-4228

LOUISIANA

4403 Veterans Memorial Blvd, Metairie, LA 70006	504-887-7631

MASSACHUSETTS

885 Providence Hwy, Dedham, MA 02026	781-326-5385

MISSOURI

9804 Watson Road, St. Louis, MO 63126	314-965-3512

NEW JERSEY

561 U.S. Route 1, Wick Plaza, Edison, NJ 08817	732-572-1200

NEW YORK

150 East 52nd Street, New York, NY 10022	212-754-1110
78 Fort Place, Staten Island, NY 10301	718-447-5071

PENNSYLVANIA

9171-A Roosevelt Blvd, Philadelphia, PA 19114	215-676-9494

SOUTH CAROLINA

243 King Street, Charleston, SC 29401	843-577-0175

TENNESSEE

4811 Poplar Avenue, Memphis, TN 38117	901-761-2987

TEXAS

114 Main Plaza, San Antonio, TX 78205	210-224-8101

VIRGINIA

1025 King Street, Alexandria, VA 22314	703-549-3806

CANADA

3022 Dufferin Street, Toronto, ON M6B 3T5	416-781-9131
1155 Yonge Street, Toronto, ON M4T 1W2	416-934-3440